Paul's Conundrum

Paul's Conundrum

*Reconciling 1 Thessalonians 2:13–16 and Romans 9:1–5
in Light of His Calling and His Heritage*

AMY KAREN DOWNEY

WIPF & STOCK · Eugene, Oregon

PAUL'S CONUNDRUM
Reconciling 1 Thessalonians 2:13–16 and Romans 9:1–5 in Light of His Calling and His Heritage

Copyright © 2011 Amy Karen Downey. All rights reserved. Except for brief quotations in critical publications or reviews, no part of this book may be reproduced in any manner without prior written permission from the publisher. Write: Permissions, Wipf and Stock Publishers, 199 W. 8th Ave., Suite 3, Eugene, OR 97401.

Third Edition (Revised)—Originally published as *Paul's Relationship to the Jewish People: An Analysis of 1 Thessalonians 2:13–16 and Romans 9:15* in two editions by Emanuel University Centre (Oradea, Romania).

Wipf & Stock
An Imprint of Wipf and Stock Publishers
199 W. 8th Ave., Suite 3
Eugene, OR 97401

www.wipfandstock.com

ISBN 13: 978-1-60899-457-1

Manufactured in the U.S.A.

*To the three men who have made an lasting impact on my life,
My father, Jack Henry Downey, who taught me to love God,
James Leo Garrett Jr., who taught me to love theology,
and Calvin Miller, who taught me that God loves it when
we seek to instill theology with imagination and creativity.*

Contents

Foreword • ix

Preface • xi

Introduction • 1

PART ONE

Introduction to Chapters 1 and 2 • 5

1   Thessalonica • 7

2   Rome • 13

PART TWO

Introduction to Chapters 3 and 4 • 21

3   Exegetical Understanding of 1 Thessalonians 2:13–16 • 23

4   Exegetical Understanding of Romans 9:1–5 • 37

PART THREE

Introduction to Chapters 5 through 7 • 59

5   Questions Regarding Interpolation and Anti-Semitism (1 Thessalonians 2:13–16) • 61

6   Rationale and Error of Dual Covenantalism (Romans 9:1–5) • 69

7   Argument of Replacement Theology (Romans 9:1–5) • 79

Conclusion • 90

Bibliography • 95

Index • 107

Foreword

WITH EXEGETICAL SKILL, THEOLOGICAL INSIGHT, and missionary passion Amy Downey has probed these two Pauline texts, which some have reckoned as contradictory (frustration as to certain judgment vs. compassion for salvation), and she does so in order to make application to the twenty-first century. First, she examines the ethnic composition of the Christian churches in Thessalonica and in Rome. In the former, Jewish Christians were seemingly a minority. In the latter, Jewish believers were the great majority until Emperor Claudius's expulsion of Jews and Jewish Christians in AD 49. The import of this difference Downey leaves to inference.

Second, the author offers an exegetical study of the two texts. According to 1 Thess 2:13–16, the Thessalonian Christians suffered from their countrymen in a manner analogous to the suffering by the churches in Judea. Indeed, the Jews are the ones who killed "the Lord Jesus" and the Old Testament prophets, such actions being displeasing to God and hostile to humanity. The divine wrath coming on such unbelieving Jews, according to Downey, is to be eschatological, though there is hope for salvation (Rom 11:26). In Rom 9:1–5 Paul, using an oath formula to speak the truth, expresses "great sorrow" and "constant distress" for his unbelieving Jewish brothers and wishes to "welcome perdition" if it could bring their salvation. Indeed, the people of Israel have had six distinct privileges plus the lineage of the fully human Messiah, who—in what is taken to be a proclamation, not a doxology—is truly God.

Third, Downey examines and finds defective three modern positions: (1) 1 Thess 2:13–16 as a "post-Pauline" "interpolation" likely expressive of Paul's anti-Semitism; (2) the modern, post-Holocaust theory of dual covenants, according to which "Gentiles are saved through Jesus and the Jews through the law of Moses"; hence, all national Israel will be eschatologically saved; and (3) replacement theology (i.e., "God has rejected the Jews as His chosen people" and replaced them with believing Gentiles), traceable to the Epistle of Barnabas and Ignatius of Antioch and in effect bringing "the spiritual genocide" of the Jewish people and making Rom 9:1–5 inexplicable.

Downey opts instead for "ethnic Israel's place in the covenant" and for salvation solely through the death and resurrection of the Messiah for both Jews and Gentiles, thus laying the foundation for an urgently needed present-day Christian witness to the Jewish people.

James Leo Garrett Jr.
Professor Emeritus
Southwestern Baptist Theological Seminary
Fort Worth, Texas

Preface

WHILE THIS WORK WAS dedicated to the three men who have had the most profound impact on my theological life, no doubt exists that the best qualities of my character have been shaped by my parents, Jack and Barbara Downey. My father, who passed away in 2000, prayed with me to receive Jesus as my Messiah. My mother illustrates to me daily the reality of a "Proverbs 31 Woman," and my spiritual growth as a Christian lady is because of her strength, wisdom, and perseverance.

I want to express my love for my sister Janice and niece Katie Hickey. Janice has illustrated a strength of character and fortitude over the past few years that is awe-inspiring. Katie continues to grow into the Christian woman that I know she can be. May God bless you both as you continue to discover God's mission plan for your lives.

This work is a revision of my MA in Theology thesis from Southwestern Baptist Theological Seminary, Fort Worth, Texas. Therefore, the best parts of this work are because of the demand for excellence insisted upon by my thesis supervisor, Dr. Siegfried Schatzmann. I cannot express fully my appreciation for his demand that I not settle for anything less than the best that God can produce in and through me. My prayer is that I have lived up to his and God's standards for excellence.

It is impossible for me to more than mention those individuals who impact my life through prayers and encouragement. I know that I will miss many people, and for that I hope to receive forgiveness and understanding. However, I must stop and thank Frank and Alice Haley, Walter and Thelma Simmons, Michael and Sharon Burchfield, Chris and Denise and Remington Price, Arnie and Barb Kupferberg, Jean Metcalf, Robin and Karen Rose, Dennis and Karen Parish, Tim and Julie Gibson, Howard and Nancy Elton, Michael and Jill Lederer, Carey and Lisa Jones, Onie Moore (1917–2010), Jack and Delores McNeeley, Nettie Tatum, George Reddin, Larry and Shawna Ashlock, James and Twyla Poe, and my students at Arlington Baptist College.

Additionally, I would like to thank my student assistant at Arlington Baptist College, James Drawbond. His work in helping me to finalize the bibliography was amazing. Cathy Drewry's work as copy editor went above and beyond the call of duty. I want to thank Professor Cornelius Simut who edited the first two editions for Emanuel University Centre in Romania. Your encouragement made it possible for me to find a publisher in America. Thank you all for your time and patience and diligence.

Many ask me why I dedicate myself to the work of Jewish evangelism and missions through Tzedakah Ministries. The obvious answer is that because of God's call on my life, I can do nothing else. A more subtle answer, and one that only a few people can understand, is because of a man named Josef Hausner. Josef's life, pain, and passing remind me that the cause of Jewish evangelism is one that must never be overlooked.

Finally, I must thank my Abba Father who called me to be His child on September 18, 1977. My daily prayer is that I will be the servant and vessel that He can utilize for His purpose for my life (Acts 20:24).

Amy Karen Downey
Tzedakah Ministries
Waxahachie, Texas
August 2010

Introduction

Aaron Burr can be described as a "man who abandoned his people," because of his traitorous actions against a fledging United States and Thomas Jefferson. He fled his livelihood and his status as vice-president after killing Alexander Hamilton in a duel. However, Aaron Burr was not the first man who could have fit the description of a man considered to be a traitor to his nation.[1]

In many ways, the Apostle Paul, who Christians hold up as the spreader of the faith to the world, was a man who lost his history and his people. When he became a believer on the Damascus Road, he abandoned everything for the faith he encountered—which while costing him his eyesight, gave him spiritual vision that was beyond 20/20. For most of Paul's post-conversion life, he was ostracized from his Temple and his legacy as a student of Gamaliel.[2] He was alienated from those he called brothers and sisters and forced to wander among the Gentiles who craved his message of Messiah Jesus.

Consequently, the letters of Paul provide insight into the thoughts, experiences, and theological development of a man who took seriously the responsibility for spreading the Gospel message of Messiah Jesus. Paul viewed his evangelistic responsibility as more than just a mere revival within Judaism itself, but a mandate that needed to be expanded to the Gentiles as well. This spiritual transformation, however, did not change Paul's ethnic identity but, in fact, Paul's Jewishness continued to be a source of personal identification and spiritual moniker for this missionary to the Gentiles (Phil 3:1–8).

The epistles of Paul illustrate to readers an individual who took his mantle as missionary to the Gentiles very seriously, yet never forgot his roots and heritage as a Jew.[3] His unique relationship with his Jewish na-

---

1. Hicks et al., *Federal Union*, 311–13.
2. Young, *Paul the Jewish Theologian*, 9, 12, 15–16, 18.
3. Murrell, "The Human Paul of the New Testament: Anti-Judaism in 1 Thess 2:14–

tion was a source of both sincere affection and acrimonious tension. This dichotomy was never more evident than in two passages, Rom 9:1–5, in which one reads of the despair Paul experienced over the spiritual condition of the Jewish people,[4] and 1 Thess 2:13–16, in which he appears to express a level of bitterness toward the Jewish people that surprises many readers.[5] These contrasting pairs of Pauline expressions,[6] along with what James Leo Garrett sees as the wide-ranging hermeneutical explanations of Rom 9–11[7] and the horrifying events of the twentieth century (i.e., the Holocaust), create the need for an adequate exegetical explanation of two passages that appear to be contradictory in intention, interpretation, and style.

PURPOSE AND APPROACHES

The purpose of this book is two-fold. First, this book seeks to examine Paul's relationship, from a positive as well as a negative perspective, with the Jewish people through an examination of two passages: Romans 9:1–5 and 1 Thessalonians 2:13–16. Second, the book hopes to discover how this relationship between Paul and the nation of Israel has impacted and continues to influence the Christian perception of and relationship with the Jewish people.

The work of resolving the two-fold purpose of this book will be achieved through three primary sections. The first section will examine

---

16," 174. Murrell, who while believing that Paul's statement in the Thessalonian passage was anti-Jewish, also stated it was not anti-Semitic. This apparent dichotomy (which will be discussed in further sections of the book) is summarized in Murrell's defense of Paul when he writes, "Paul's emphasis is not race or ethnic prejudice" (174).

4. Hagner, "Paul's Quarrel with Judaism," 131; and Jewett, "The Law and Coexistence of Jews and Gentiles in Romans," 343.

5. Wortham, "The Problem of Anti-Judaism in 1 Thess. 2:14–16 and Related Pauline Texts," 37. Wortham described this passage as "may be the earliest example of anti-Judaism in Second Testament." See also Meeks, *The Writings of St. Paul: A Norton Critical Edition*, 6.

6. Jewett, "Law and Coexistence of Jews and Gentiles in Romans," 343; and Murrell, "Human Paul of the New Testament," 174. This dichotomy of expressions caused many theologians to grasp for explanations regarding Paul's attitudes toward himself as a Jew and the Jewish people in general. Robert Jewett (343) explored this confusion as he compared the passage in question to the accusations of anti-Judaism (a rejection of Judaism "as a religious community") made by such biblical scholars as Rosemary Radford Ruether. Ruether, *Faith and Fratricide: The Theological Roots of Anti-Semitism*, 104.

7. Garrett, *Systematic Theology*, 2:440.

the historical backgrounds of the Thessalonian and Roman churches and how the ethnic composition of the two churches might have impacted the tone and manner Paul utilized in responding to the spiritual needs and concerns of the Jewish people. For example, the church of Thessalonica found itself in a city that was cosmopolitan in nature, much as Rome itself was, and was one of the centers of Caesar worship.[8] This diversity of people groups created a Thessalonian church that was primarily Gentile in nature and focus.[9] Additionally, the church at Thessalonica overcame persecution, which is crucial to understanding and analyzing 1 Thess 2:13–16, and the church became a witness of faithfulness to Christ to other Macedonian believers of the first century[10] and to the worldwide Christian church of today.

In contrast, the Roman Church, at least until the expulsion of Jews from the city of Rome in AD 49, and their subsequent readmission in AD 54 by Nero, was comprised primarily of a significant number of Jewish believers.[11] Therefore, it may be argued—an issue that will be explored in the book—that even though Paul wrote the epistle to the Romans almost a decade after the Jewish expulsion (AD 55–57),[12] the vestiges of Jewish influence could still have impacted the tone and manner of Paul's letter to the Roman church.

The second section in developing an answer to the book question will analyze and compare/contrast the exegetical significance of the two passages. This analysis of Rom 9:1–5 and 1 Thess 2:13–16 will examine the passages in light of both the context and the intended purpose of the Pauline statements. Paul's personal relationship with the Jewish people, and how this impacted both passages, will also be examined. Questions will be examined, such as: (1) was the relationship between Paul and the Jewish people one of genuine compassion and lament, as found in Rom 9:1–5? or, (2) was it the case in 1 Thess 2:13–16 of Paul expressing a very human emotion that was not sanctioned or ordained by God?[13]

---

8. Tellbe, *Paul Between Synagogue and State*, 80–86.

9. Taylor, "Who Persecuted the Thessalonian Christians?" 784; and Still, *Conflict at Thessalonica*, 65.

10. Milligan, *St. Paul's Epistle to the Thessalonians*, 27.

11. Walters, *Ethnic Issues in Paul's Letter to the Romans*, 56–57, 58; Bell, *Provoked to Jealousy*, 64–66, 67–68, 72, 76–77; and Dunn, "Romans, Letter to the," 839.

12. Bell, *Provoked to Jealousy*, 68–69, 78; and Dunn, "Romans, Letter to the," 839.

13. Gager, *The Origins of Anti-Semitism: Attitudes Toward Judaism in Pagan and Christian Antiquity*, 256.

The third section to answering the questions presented in this book will be through an examination of the theological significance that these two passages have had for the Christian church, past and present, and its relationship to its Jewish heritage. The three focal areas will include: (1) answering the question regarding accusations that Paul was an anti-Semite[14] (or self-hating Jew);[15] (2) the rationale of dual covenantalism;[16] and (3) the argument both for and against replacement, or supercessionist, theology.[17]

Even while analyzing 1 Thess 2:13–16 and Rom 9:1–5, this book ultimately will seek to answer an almost impossible series of questions. Did this consequence of being an outcast create for Paul a self-hatred of his ethnicity? Did he respond to the hatred with his own form of hatred? This book, *Paul's Conundrum*, will seek to answer not only these questions, but also to discover a way to reconcile two seemingly contradictory passages that create confusion as Paul's feelings toward his own people. For when contradiction is reconciled, the next question must be: What was Paul's ultimate longing for his own people? This truly is the ultimate conundrum.

---

14. Klassen, "Anti-Judaism in Early Christianity," 16. The issue of accusations of anti-Semitic behavior by Paul is a matter of discussion that will be analyzed more fully in the book. However, it is important to note that views on this question reflect a variety of opinions, regardless of a theologian's own personal liberal, moderate, or conservative perspective.

15. Telushkin, *Jewish Literacy*, 472–74. Rabbi Telushkin defined a "self-hating Jew" as someone who both considers the Jewish people as somewhat lesser than other peoples and nations and is a Jewish person who turns against his or her own people.

16. Beker, "Romans 9–11 in the Context of the Early Church," 45. Scholars and theologians who hold to a dual covenant theology often see the Romans 9 passage (as well as chapters 10 and 11), as evidence of God's confirmation as cited by Beker that "the eschatological destiny of Israel" would be evidenced "at the time of the eschatological triumph of God."

17. Barth, *The Epistle to the Romans*, 332, 334–35, 337. Barth (332) writes, "And now, in contrast with the Gospel of Jesus Christ, there is thrust upon our attention—Israel, the Church, the world of religion as it appears in history, and we hasten to add, Israel in its purest, truest, and most powerful aspect." See also, Hall, *Christian Anti-Semitism and Paul's Theology*, 116. Hall cited Augustine as an illustration of how the concept of replacement theology came to the forefront. For example, Augustine compared the Jewish people to the Witness People (as opposed to Chosen People) who were doomed to be witnesses of what happens when one rejects Jesus, and that they are nothing more than "Christ-killers." A modern conservative and evangelical advocate of a modified replacement theology is perhaps found in the writings of John MacArthur. MacArthur sees the Rom 9:1–5 passage as evidence that the Jewish people have been "temporarily set aside by God" so that the Lord could accomplish His divine plan for humanity. See MacArthur, *MacArthur New Testament Commentary Romans 9–16*, 6.

PART ONE

Introduction to Chapters 1 and 2

Depending on one's viewpoint, when it came to their children, my parents were either the luckiest parents in the world or good-natured masochists due to the continual purchase of compact vehicles. My sister and I had the normal sibling relationship. We loved each other, and we fought a lot. However, it was the family car trip that exemplified our relationship.

We fought over such catastrophic issues as "her hair is on my side of the car," or "she is breathing my share of the air." We then fell asleep with my sister's head in my lap, and with my head on her hipbone. We also liked to sing songs. We did not sing "100 Bottles of Beer on the Wall," for my father was a pastor. We sang the theme song to the old television show "Green Acres," and we sang it for many, many miles.

Little did we realize then that this theme song would epitomize our adult personalities. She likes the country. I like the city. She loves "roughing it." I consider it a primitive adventure to stay in a motel with one-ply toilet paper. She hunts for the elusive 10-point buck in a deer stand. I hunt for rare finds in a musty and dusty bookstore. Yet, we share the same genetic make-up from our parents, we look remarkably alike for sisters almost five years apart, and we were even Rh-factor babies due to our blood types being O+, while our mother's was O-.

Two cities are under consideration, which are somewhat parallel to the relationship between my sister and myself, specifically as it relates to what they illustrate about Paul's relationship with the Jewish people. Thessalonica was an important port city in Asia Minor. Rome was the center of the world. Thessalonica was primarily Gentile in ethnic flavor. Rome was a cultural "melting pot." Thessalonica sought the approval of the emperors. Rome was the home of the emperors. However, the recipients of the two Pauline letters possessed the common genetic spiritual factor of being followers of Messiah Jesus, and being relatively new in the faith. Therefore, to understand why Paul's consideration of the Jewish people was seemingly in diametrical mutual opposition is important. Thus, this is where our census of the two cities begins. . . .

1

Thessalonica

THE LETTERS TO THE churches in Thessalonica and Rome were uniquely original in content and approach. The tone and focus of each epistle reflected the cultural and political tenor of the cities. The epistles provide insight into the theological nuances of uniquely different churches, which Paul confronted and attempted to resolve. In Thessalonians, a reader seems to find a caustic diatribe in his attitude and condemnation of the people from which he comes genetically.

HISTORICAL BACKGROUND OF THE CITY

In Thessalonica, Paul encountered a city that, while founded in 316 BC,[1] was thoroughly enraptured with playing the role of a major city of the Roman Empire.[2] Their dedication to the worship of Caesar (Acts 17:7)[3] and its place as a major conduit for trade on the Via Egnatia exemplified this philosophy.[4] Thessalonica was a city hesitant to do anything to ham-

---

1. Still, *Conflict at Thessalonica*, 63; and Meeks, *First Urban Christians*, 46. See also Tod, "Thessalonica," in *ISBE*. Tod explains the founding of the city as occurring when Antipater, the king of Macedonia, consolidated various surrounding villages into one larger cosmopolitan area.

2. Brisco, *Holman Bible Atlas*, 193. Brisco notes that Thessalonica was conquered by the Romans during the Macedonian Wars and the ultimate defeat of Philip V in 197 BC.

3. Manus, "Luke's Account of Paul," 28; and Donfried, "Cults of Thessalonica," 337–46.

4. Grant, *World of Rome*, 31; Manus, "Luke's Account of Paul," 28; and Meeks, *First Urban Christians*, 46. Wayne Meeks notes that Thessalonica and Corinth were considered the two most important trading cities of "Roman Greece."

per its important status in the Roman Empire,[5] even among the hodgepodge of religious idols and concepts.[6]

This sense of status consciousness,[7] regardless of ethnicity or religious preference, is best understood through the Thessalonian "decrees of Caesar."[8] In fact, these decrees are what many scholars (including E. A. Judge and J. R. Harrison) believe to be the charges laid against Jason and the Thessalonian Christians in Acts 17.[9] According to Todd Still, the reason for these charges is because of the perception that Paul's teaching was an attempt to offer an alternative to Caesar worship, which would not only be seditious, but also heresy to the Roman Empire.[10]

---

5. Tellbe, *Paul Between Synagogue and State*, 80–86; Taylor, "Who Persecuted the Thessalonian Christians?," 791; Donfried, *Paul, Thessalonica, and Early Christianity*, 22–38, esp. 31–38, 140–43; Manus, "Luke's Account of Paul," 28; and Meeks, *First Urban Christians*, 47. Manus describes Thessalonica "as a center of Roman administration, a center of Hellenistic civilization, and a center of Jewish influence." Meeks notes that Thessalonica was named the capital of the Macdeonian province in 146 BC.

6. Donfried, "Cults of Thessalonica," 337–46; and Manus, "Luke's Account of Paul," 28. Donfried highlights the various religious cults of the Thessalonians, including the worship of Serapis, Isis, Dionysus, and Cabirus. Dionysus was the cult for those involved heavily in sexual practices and variations, while Cabirus, though sexual in practice due to its phallic symbolism, relied more heavily on its history of how the cult began—fratricide through two brothers killing the third and placing his head at the foot of Mount Olympus.

7. Donfried, *Paul, Thessalonica, and Early Christianity*, 35. Karl Donfried provides a brief overview for the lofty status of Thessalonica and possible reasons why the city was so uncomfortable with the tumult that Paul was causing with his preaching of the Gospel. One of the key points for why Thessalonica was considered a "free city" is the appreciation of the empire for their support of Antony and Octavian (the future Caesar Augustus) in the battle against Brutus.

8. Judge, "Decrees of Caesar at Thessalonica," 1–7, esp. 2, 5, and 7. Judge notes that the alleged violations of the decrees of Caesar are not specified, but rather lie in the concept that Paul was presenting another king worthy of worship. See also Harrison, "Paul and the Imperial Gospel," 80–82; and Wanamaker, *Epistles to the Thessalonians*, 113–14.

9. Taylor, "Who Persecuted the Thessalonian Christians?," 791; Still, *Conflict at Thessalonica*, 76. Still believes the accusations against Jason and the Christ followers to be ones of sedition. A contrary view is presented by Manus, "Luke's Account of Paul," 33, who believes that the charges in Acts 17 are a "free Lucan composition," in other words an addition for dramatic effect. Obviously, the idea that Luke would be granted "free license" in his writing of Acts requires one to be on the more liberal spectrum end of the inerrancy debate.

10. Still, *Conflict at Thessalonica*, 77. Still believes primarily that the "eschatological elements" in Paul's sermons most unsettled the citizens of Thessalonica.

Consequently, Ernest Best believes that the opponents to Paul's witness of Christ, as found in Acts 17 and 1 Thess 2:13–16, should not be limited simply to one group of individuals. Best believes it was not just worshippers of the emperors. He expands the group to include everyone, from Hellenistic Jews to skeptical Thessalonians, who were wary that Paul was simply the next "wandering teacher," teaching only for the purpose of stirring up controversy.[11] If stirred up enough, controversy would bring reproach upon the people of the city.

However, N. H. Taylor has questioned the possibility of a significant Jewish population, because no archaeological excavation of Thessalonica has resulted in the discovery of a synagogue.[12] Ernst Haenchen takes the opposing view to Taylor by advocating that the reality of Thessalonica's place as a major city in the Roman Empire by *de facto* evidence requires the presence of a Jewish population and synagogue.[13] The Jewish population of Thessalonica, according to Todd Still, would have been present in the city at around AD 50, due to the "wide dispersion of Jews throughout the eastern half of the Roman empire," and because of its role as a "heavily populated port city."[14] Therefore, the rationale for a Jewish population in Thessalonica, as reflected in the passage in question, is based on credible evidence as well as scriptural tradition.[15]

---

11. Best, *First and Second Epistles to the Thessalonians*, 16–22 (page citations are to the reprint edition). See also Huidekoper, *Judaism at Rome*, 233.

12. Taylor, "Who Persecuted the Thessalonian Christians?" 789.

13. Haenchen, *Acts of the Apostles*, 6; Wanamaker, *Epistles to the Thessalonians*, 4; Manus, "Luke's Account of Paul," 32; and Meeks, *First Urban Christians*, 46. Meeks, 46, does not rely on inferred rational evidence for his support of the view that a synagogue existed in Thessalonica, but rather the recent archaeological uncovering of synagogal evidence in Stobi, located near Thessalonica.

14. Still, *Conflict at Thessalonica*, 63–64, 150–65.

15. Holtz, "Judgment on the Jews and the Salvation of All Israel," 284–85; Donfried, "Cults of Thessalonica," 128–29, 201–5. Donfried spends a significant amount of time and thought on a comparison of the sufferings of the Judean church at the malevolent hands of Jewish leaders, as opposed to the suffering of the Thessalonian church by the devices of Thessalonian Jews. In fact, Donfried, "Cults of Thessalonica," 201, states that, in order to develop a better exegetical understanding of 1 Thessalonians 2, one must see its relevance to Acts 17.

INTRODUCTION TO THE THESSALONIAN CHURCH

Ethnic Composition of the Church

The traditional understanding of the ethnic composition of the church at Thessalonica is that it was almost overwhelmingly Gentile.[16] The Thessalonian Jews did not respond to the message of the Messiahship of Jesus, presented by Paul when he first entered the city. A variety of reasons are possible for this lack of responsiveness and eventual antagonism, including the proposal that the Jewish leaders were jealous of Paul's apparent ability to attract former God-fearers, and possibly even Jewish women, to the message of the resurrected Messiah.[17] This lack of Jewish representation in the Thessalonian church perhaps offers a possible reason why Paul's words, regarding Jewish opponents to the Gospel, were untempered and apparently unedited.

Establishment of the Church

The beginnings of the church at Thessalonica are rooted in Paul's second missionary journey (Acts 15:36—18:22)[18] and follow his liberation from prison and the salvation of the jailor and his family at Philippi (Acts 16:19–40).[19] In the establishment of the Thessalonian church, Paul followed one of his church-planting patterns (Acts 17:2) of going first to the Jews (on the Sabbath and in their own synagogue), when a Jewish community was present. Only after suffering rejection by the Jewish citizens of the city did Paul present the Gospel message to the Gentiles.[20]

---

16. Still, *Conflict at Thessalonica*, 65.

17. Still, *Conflict at Thessalonica*, 69–71. Still (p. 153–65) notes the possible hypocritical reaction to those Jewish individuals who considered Paul as a traitor to Judaism, especially in light of their own apparent drift away from the core tenets of Judaism, including the disregard of dietary laws and intermarriage with Gentiles.

18. Tod, "Thessalonica," in *ISBE*.

19. Walker, "Thessalonians, The First Epistle," in *ISBE*; and, Still, "Paul's Thessalonian Mission," 10–11.

20. Taylor, "Who Persecuted the Thessalonian Christians?," 796; Donfried, *Paul, Thessalonica, and Early Christianity*, 94; Garrett, *Systematic Theology*, 2:493–95; Still, "Paul's Thessalonian Mission," 11; Walker, "Thessalonians, The First Epistle," in *ISBE*; and Hiebert, *Thessalonian Epistles*, 15. Todd Still presents, but discounts, the alternate position of the concept that Paul went first to the synagogue in Thessalonica. The rationale for this anti-synagogal argument as merely a "Lukan stylization" is because Still believes it contradicts the Gentile emphasis of Paul's mission. Still, *Conflict at Thessalonica*, 64.

The duration of Paul's time in Thessalonica is subject to interpretation, as some advocate an initial church establishment period of longer than three weeks, due to the level of loyalty and intensity exhibited by Jason and others when the leaders of the city came to arrest Paul and Silas (Acts 17).[21] The length of Paul's initial stay[22] is not critical to understanding the relationship between Paul and the Christians of Thessalonica. The importance of the relationship between the Thessalonian church and Paul was the depth of love and commitment that remained constant, regardless of the other's circumstances.

Provenance and Purpose of 1 Thessalonians

Paul writes his letter to the church after hearing Timothy's account of his visit with them (1 Thess 3:2, 6). After receiving the news of their faithfulness and steadfastness to the Gospel, Paul responds with joy and praise.[23] The letter to the Thessalonians focuses more on encouragement and spiritual growth,[24] and not on doctrinal issues, except as it pertains to eschatology (chapter 4).

This interrelationship of devotion and loyalty between Paul and the Thessalonian church is one of the reasons why almost universal agreement exists among conservative scholars that the letter(s) to the Thessalonians was the first penned by Paul from the city of Corinth in AD 50 or 51.[25] In his commentary on 1 and 2 Thessalonians, I. Howard Marshall does not provide an exact date, as he notes that a few scholars state that the epistles to the Thessalonians should receive a later date—perhaps being written as late as the third missionary journey.[26]

---

21. Still, *Conflict at Thessalonica*, 67.

22. Alternative views regarding the duration of Paul's tenure in Thessalonica expand for some scholars beyond three weeks to anywhere from one to three months. Wanamaker, *Epistles to the Thessalonians*, 7; and Malherbe, *Paul and the Thessalonians*, 62–63.

23. Hiebert, *Thessalonian Epistles*, 21, 25.

24. Green, *Letters to the Thessalonians*, 56; and Best, *First and Second Epistles to the Thessalonians*, 15.

25. Williams, *1 and 2 Thessalonians*, 10; Bockmuehl, "1 Thessalonians 2:14–16 and the Church in Jerusalem," 17–18; Bruce, *1 & 2 Thessalonians*, xxxiv–xxxv; Gilliard, "Paul and the Killing of the Prophets," 259; Hiebert, *Thessalonian Epistles*, 25; Tellbe, *Paul Between Synagogue and State*, 80; Taylor, "Who Persecuted the Thessalonian Christians?," 786; and, Best, *First and Second Epistles to the Thessalonians*, 11.

26. Marshall, *1 and 2 Thessalonians*, 21–22.

Karl Donfried provides one of the earliest dates for the writing of the epistle—AD 43. He bases his rationale upon the view that Claudius expelled Jews from Rome in AD 41 and the dating of the Jerusalem Conference as AD 51–52.[27] Charles Wanamaker focuses his discussion regarding the dating of 1 and 2 Thessalonians, not so much on when the letters were written, but on the order in which they were penned. He concludes that 2 Thessalonians was actually written first.[28] Additionally, 1 Thessalonians is recognized as being Pauline in nature and authorship, with the recognition that Paul wrote this epistle as almost universal in nature.[29]

CONCLUDING THOUGHTS ON THE CHURCH AT THESSALONICA

Thessalonica was not an atypical church plant for Paul. The people were different. The needs were different. The lack of Jewish believers in the congregation changed its perspective and allegiance. Perhaps, this was even one of the first churches to forget the Jewish background of its faith. While this supposition is merely a guess, the antagonism toward the Jewish people in the city of Thessalonica continues to this day with the recent attack on a Hebrew cemetery in Thessaloniki (modern-day name variation) that desecrated the final resting places of dozens of Jewish graves.[30] Was the attack the result of the renewed rise of Neo-Nazi-style tactics, or rather something that has been festering in its citizens' DNA for almost two thousand years? Is Paul responsible for this latest incarnation of anti-Semitism? Or does its hatred find its roots in another source more sinister than a reading of Paul's word to a church almost two millennia old?

---

27. Donfried, *Paul, Thessalonica, and Early Christianity*, 74–76. Donfried bases his argument for this date upon Paul's initial encounter with Aquila and Priscilla who, while citizens of Rome, were living in Corinth due to Claudius's act of expulsion (Acts 18:1–2).

28. Wanamaker, *Epistles to the Thessalonians*, 37–45.

29. Wanamaker, *Epistles to the Thessalonians*, 17–29; Best, *First and Second Epistles to the Thessalonians*, 25–26; and, Green, *Letter to the Thessalonians*, 54–55. Green utilizes external historical sources as additional proofs for Pauline authorship, including the testimonies of Ignatius, Tertullian, Eusebius, and even Marcion. Further, he mentions extrabiblical epistles such as *Didache* and *Shepherd of Hermas* that cite 1 Thessalonians as circumstantial evidence for proof of the Pauline authorship claim for the epistle.

30. Henry Papachristou and Dina Kyriakidou, "Vandals Desecrate Jewish Cemetery in Greece," Internet.

2

Rome

The epistle to the Roman church appears on the surface to be 180-degree polar opposite from the letters to the church at Thessalonica. In this posting to "the saints," we find a Paul who exhibits an almost fatherly lament regarding the eternal salvation of the Jewish people. We see a prioritization of Jewish evangelization in Romans 1:16. We see a section (chapters 9–11) focused on the eternal destiny of his brothers and sisters.

Does a reason exist for this apparent opposite reaction? Was Paul in a "bad mood" when he wrote to the Thessalonian church? Or, does the reason lie in the fact that Paul was writing to a completely different audience from the one found in Thessalonica?

HISTORICAL BACKGROUND OF THE CITY

The heart and soul of the empire, the place where the philosophy of *Pax Romana* ("Roman peace") was born, is the city of Rome. The city, according to tradition, was founded by Romulus in 753 BC, and influenced by the Etruscans in the mid-to-late-600s.[1] According to Thomas Brisco, the Republic began around 509 BC.

Interestingly enough, the Republic–while hesitant to have a king rule over the people–still practiced a form of oligarchy, the rule of the elite.[2] The beginning stages of the Roman Empire are visible as early as the Early Republic (c.510–264 BC).[3] This city-state grew in power and prestige

---

1. Brisco, *Holman Bible Atlas*, 190.
2. Brisco, *Holman Bible Atlas*, 190.
3. Westenholz, ed. *Jewish Presence*, 14.

during the various phases of the Republic,[4] and perhaps fully realized its dynastic potential with the reign of Julius Caesar (c. 49–44 BC).[5]

The presence and impact of the Jewish people in the Roman Empire, and in Rome itself, are defined by various historians in different ways. Some assume that a Jewish contingency first arrived in Rome during the beginning days of the Hasmonean dynasty in 161 BC.[6] In fact, indications in 1 Maccabees 8 are that Judah the Hammer sent an envoy to Rome in order to establish diplomatic relations.[7]

Erich S. Gruen believes that the first foray of Jewish culture and influence was seen in Rome as early as c.400 BC because of an order by either Julius Paris or Cornelius Hispalus that the Chaldeans and the Jews had to leave Rome due to their "heretical" religious teachings.[8] However, and regardless of the actual beginning date for a Jewish presence in the Italian peninsula, the strongest evidence for the first major Jewish presence to be found in Rome is the c.161 BC date for one primary reason–the lack of evidence beyond that of Erich Gruen's speculation regarding an expulsion in 400 BC.

The first date that one can point to with certainty for a Jewish population in Rome is 139 BC, as this is the established date of their first expulsion from the capital of the Roman Empire.[9] The rationale for a Jewish expulsion from Rome in 139 BC can be traced back to one basic and primary factor—the desire to expand the Jewish faith to greater regions and influence.[10] This influence of Jewish faith and practice created a sense of political, religious, and social instability that Rome could not tolerate.

---

4. Grant, *World of Rome*, 3. Michael Grant notes that the growth of the Roman Empire truly began around 241 BC when its power and influence expanded beyond the peninsula to the rest of the world.

5. Westenholz, ed. *Jewish Presence*, 14.

6. Westenholz, ed. *Jewish Presence*, 14, 17; Brändle and Stegemann, "Formation of the First 'Christian Congregations' in Rome," 119; and Sanday and Headlam, *Epistle to the Romans*, xix.

7. Westenholz, ed., *Jewish Presence*, 17. Additionally, Westenholz notes the probability of additional diplomatic forays to Rome in c.150 and c.139 BC.

8. Gruen, *Diaspora*, 16.

9. Westenholz, ed. *Jewish Presence*, 14; Brändle and Stegemann, "Formation of the First 'Christian Congregations' in Rome," 119; and Grant, *World of Rome*, 44.

10. Westenholz, ed. *Jewish Presence*, 18; Walters, *Ethnic Issues*, 38; Leon, *Jews of Ancient Rome*, 2–3; and Ferguson, *Religions of the Roman Empire*, 88–98, esp. 95.

The next certain date for a Jewish presence in Rome was during the forced emigration of many Judeans during the Roman takeover of the Jewish state by Pompey in 63 BC.[11] In fact, a Jewish presence in Rome survived the assassination of Julius Caesar and additional expulsions, such as the one in AD 19 that was due to a perceived manipulation of a Roman citizen by two Jewish "con artists."[12] James Walters even estimates that approximately ten years before the death of Jesus in Jerusalem, the Jewish population in Rome could have exceeded forty thousand.[13] The potential explanation for such a large Jewish population in Rome can be attributed to the number of Jewish slaves who were brought after Pompey's military campaigns in Syria and Judea.[14]

Therefore, and regardless of the actual size of the Jewish population, it is safe to assume that a Jewish community was present in Rome during the reign of Emperor Claudius.[15] However, it was also during the reign of Claudius that another edict of expulsion came down against both Messianic and non-Messianic Jews. The expulsion of the Jews from Rome in AD 49[16] has been attributed to the statement *impulsore Chresto assidue tumultuantes Roma expulit* ("He [Claudius] drove them out, [because

---

11. Westenholz, ed. *Jewish Presence*, 14, 18; Grant, *World of Rome*, 9, 44; Gruen, *Diaspora*, 16; Cary and Scullard, *History of Rome*, 198–99; Rutgers, "Roman Policy Toward the Jews," 97; Leon, *Jews of Ancient Rome*, 4–5; and Bruce, "Romans Debate," 339.

12. Rutgers, "Roman Policy Toward the Jews," 99–100, 102–3; and Grant, *World of Rome*, 44–45. Leonard Rutgers highlights the actions of the con artists who allegedly deceived Fulvia, a proselyte, by taking her offering for the temple and using it for themselves. Regardless of the legitimacy of the traditional account of expulsion, Rutgers notes the growing concern among the empire of the influence of Judaism and its missionary zeal for conversions. See also Cary and Scullard, *History of Rome*, 400.

13. Walters, *Ethnic Issues*, 28–29. An alternative population figure is provided by Brändle and Stegemann, "Formation of the First 'Christian Congregations' in Rome," 120, which estimates the figure to be less than ten thousand during the reign of Augustus. Gruen, *Diaspora*, 15, estimates between twenty thousand and sixty thousand, but leans toward the smaller number.

14. Johnson, "Jews and Christians in Rome," 52; and Rutgers, "Roman Policy Toward the Jews," 97–98. Rutgers does not provide an exact population figure; however, he does state that "not [an] inconsiderable number of Jews in Rome had become *cives Romani* [Roman citizens] by the time of Augustus from their participation in the monthly doles."

15. Bell, *Provoked to Jealousy*, 64–66; and Dunn, "Romans, Letter to the," 839.

16. Westenholz, ed. *Jewish Presence*, 14; Gruen, *Diaspora*, 39–41; Bruce, "The Romans Debate—Continued," 338–39; and Lampe, *From Paul to Valentinus*, 12.

they were] constantly in an uproar at the instigation of Chrestus").[17] For many, this edict has been seen as a response to the impact that Christianity was having on the citizens of Rome,[18] including both Jewish and Gentile citizens.[19] Among those who were expelled from Rome were the husband and wife team of Aquila and Priscilla, who had a strong influence on the life and ministry of Paul in such places as Corinth and Ephesus (Acts 18:1–4; 1 Cor 16:19; Rom 16:3; and 2 Tim 4:19).[20]

Following the death of Claudius in AD 54, and the beginning of the reign of Nero (AD 54–68),[21] Jewish Christians and traditional non-Messianic Jews were allowed to return to Rome. By this time, Jewish believers were now outnumbered by Gentile Christians, resulting in both conflict and confusion for the Church itself.[22] The spiritual and cultural climate of the Roman church, with its diverse ethnic configuration, was such that Paul addressed both the Jewish and the Gentile membership regarding the equality they could find through their joint relationship with Christ.[23] This reality, which Paul noted, provides a special poignancy (as will be seen in the exegetical chapter on Rom 9:1–5) to the heartbreak Paul

---

17. Translation provided by Dr. Robert Bernard of Southwestern Baptist Theological Seminary, Fort Worth, Texas.

18. The general assumption is that while, and even though, the word in Latin is *Chrestus* instead of *Christus*, the edict of Claudius was in response to the influence that the "Christ-followers" were having on the city of Rome. See Walters, *Ethnic Issues*, 52; Lampe, *From Paul to Valentinus*, 11–13; Brändle and Stegemann, "Formation of the First 'Christian Congregations' in Rome," 118; Bruce, "The Romans Debate—Continued," 339–40; and Leon, *Jews of Ancient Rome*, 23–26.

19. Walters, *Ethnic Issues*, 56–57; Sanday and Headlam, *Epistle to the Romans*, xxi; Stuhlmacher, *Paul's Letter to the Romans*, 6–8.

20. Walters, *Ethnic Issues*, 58; and Bell, *Provoked to Jealousy*, 67–68, 72, 76–77.

21. Stuhlmacher, *Paul's Letter to the Romans*, 7.

22. Williamson, *Has God Rejected His People*, 59; Bruce, *Letter of Paul to the Romans*, 172–73; Bell, *Provoked to Jealousy*, 70–71; and Walters, *Ethnic Issues*, 56–58. One of the primary differences is that both Walters and Bell note that the church itself has moved from a synagogue setting to a house-church environment. Further, Bell notes that, even though many of the Gentile Christians had originally been God-fearers, Jewish believers likely still struggled with old-class prejudices. God-fearers were considered "second class" at best in the Temple era, and hence a possible reason why Paul felt the necessity to emphasize the lack of "distinction between Jew and Gentile" (3:22; 10:12).

23. Stowers, *Rereading of Romans*, 287; Jewett, "Law and the Coexistence of Jews and Gentiles," 349; Gager, *Reinventing Paul*, 106–7; and Williamson, *Has God Rejected His People*, 59.

expresses over the spiritual condition of the majority of the Jewish people in Rome and throughout the Empire.

INTRODUCTION TO THE ROMAN CHURCH

Establishment of the Church

The actual date for the founding of the Church at Rome is a matter of some dispute, as is the identity of the church planter. To a large extent, this confusion depends upon an individual's denominational preference. While discounting the traditional Catholic view that Peter founded the church in Rome during the reign of Claudius in AD 49, William G. T. Shedd notes that the historical precedence for the Roman Catholic view rests upon the ambiguous testimony of Eusebius.[24] A more Protestant understanding of the Roman church's founding is that it was established as a result of the testimony of Jewish believers who traveled to Rome from the Middle East[25] in the mid to late-40s AD.[26] In other words, for some Protestants, neither Peter nor Paul had a role in the founding of the congregation in Rome.[27]

Regardless of the difference of opinions of how the Roman church began, evangelical agreement holds that the church itself began among the Jewish people of Rome and in the synagogues of Hellenistic Jews.[28] The synagogues of Rome played an important role, not only in the continuation of Jewish history for these Hellenized Roman Jews,[29] but also as a

---

24. Shedd, *Commentary on Romans*, 2. In his writings, Shedd goes on to provide five reasons why it would have been impossible for Peter to have been "the first Bishop of Rome."

25. Bell, *Provoked to Jealousy*, 64–66; Johnson, "Jews and Christians in Rome," 52; and Sanday and Headlam, *Epistle to the Romans*, xxv–xxvi.

26. Walters, *Ethnic Issues*, 56–58; and Cary and Scullard, *History of Rome*, 401.

27. Walters, *Ethnic Issues*, 63.

28. Walters, *Ethnic Issues*, 57; Bruce, "Romans Debate," 338; Brändle and Stegemann, "Formation of the First 'Christian Congregations' in Rome," 122; and Lampe, *From Paul to Valentinus*, 12.

29. Johnson, "Jews and Christians in Rome," 52; and Westenholz, ed. *Jewish Presence*, 23–27. Westenholz mentions briefly the following synagogues as important to Roman Jewish history—Augusteneses which was probably the oldest synagogue in Rome; Agrippenses which was possibly named after the son-in-law of Augustus who was known to be a friend of the Jews, Herodienses, Campenses, Siburenses, Calcarenses, Elea, Tripolitani, Sekenoi, Arca of Lebanon, Hebraei, and Vernaculi.

place from which the Christian church could expand and grow.[30] However, it was also in these same synagogues that the eventual rivalry between traditional Judaism and the Jewish sect, eventually known as Christianity, began and festered. Many believe this rivalry held the root causes for the edict of expulsion of all Jews from Rome by Emperor Claudius.[31]

Ethnic Composition of the Church

According to James Walters, charter members of the Roman church were either Jewish believers and/or God-fearing Gentiles (Jewish proselytes) who became Christians after the Gospel had spread to Rome.[32] This power structure, in which Jewish Christians were the majority members of the Roman church, obviously changed during and after the expulsion of the Jews from Rome in AD 49.[33] Upon the return of the Jewish Christians to Rome in AD 54, the church was not as it had once been. The absence of a Jewish Christian presence allowed Gentile Christians to establish a strong foothold in the Roman church. Upon the return of Jewish Christians in AD 54, this power shift created cultural and theological issues that Paul sought to resolve in his letter.[34]

Provenance and Purpose of Romans

Even though the purpose of Romans is subject to various views and opinions, the primary and prevailing view is that the epistle was written as a continuation of Paul's missionary expression and endeavor to the Gentile world. Adolf Schlatter views this outreach to the Gentile world as the spreading of the righteousness of God, despite the negative Jewish community's reaction to Paul's message.[35]

---

30. Walters, *Ethnic Issues*, 63–64; Lampe, *From Paul to Valentinus*, 12, 14–15; and Bruce, "Romans Debate," 338.

31. Bruce, "Romans Debate," 338–39; and Lampe, *From Paul to Valentinus*, 14–15.

32. Walters, *Ethnic Issues*, 57. See also Brändle and Stegemann, "Formation of the First 'Christian Congregations' in Rome," 118; and Lampe, *From Paul to Valentinus*, 69–70, 72.

33. Lampe, *From Paul to Valentinus*, 74, 158; and Brändle and Stegemann, "Formation of the First 'Christian Congregations' in Rome," 124.

34. Bruce, "Romans Debate," 340–41; and Walters, *Ethnic Issues*, 58.

35. Schlatter, *Romans*, 19–20. See also Stuhlmacher, *Paul's Letter to the Romans*, 10–11.

Further, scholars promote the classical view that Romans is the *magnum opus*, or comprehensive theological statement, of Paul's doctrine and faith.[36] However, a more developed and nuanced understanding for the purpose of the epistle is to see that many purposes and aims exist for the epistle,[37] including—but not limited to—a call for the Roman church to take on the responsibility and obligation of Jewish evangelism (Rom 1:16; 9:1—11:36). In other words, and because of such passages as Rom 1:16 and chapters 9-11, after the expulsion edict of Claudius, the primarily Gentile church still needed to remember the Jewish roots of its founding. This remembrance, as will be expanded upon in chapter 3, would enable both the Jewish and Gentile membership to be united as one in Christ.

Proof of Pauline Authorship

This attention to the Jewish heritage of the Roman church is one of the reasons why the traditional view of Pauline authorship of the Epistle is considered dominant.[38] However, Joseph Fitzmyer notes that some theologians have attempted to dispute the concept of Pauline authorship in all or parts of the epistle, primarily due to the insertion of Tertius's note in 16:22.[39] However, Fitzmyer's speculation[40] is based more on assumption than on solid, rational evidence, and the consensus view of Pauline

---

36. Sneen, "Root, the Remnant, and the Branches," 398; Stuhlmacher, *Paul's Letter to the Romans*, 3, 6; Beker, "Faithfulness of God," 11; Gager, *Reinventing Paul*, 101–3; and Shedd, *Commentary on Romans*, 4–5. Interestingly enough, both Shedd and Stuhlmacher note that another probable purpose for the writing of the epistle is to deliver a "polemic against Judaism." However, Gager, while agreeing with Shedd and Stuhlmacher that a prominent Jewish aspect related to the Epistle is present, disagrees with them and believes that the purpose for the epistle is related to the purpose he had for the epistle to the Galatian churches (cf. Gal 1:2).

37. Morris, *Epistle to the Romans*, 7–17; and Dunn, "Romans, Letter to the," 839–41. Dunn limits the purposes for the epistle to three–missionary, apologetic, and pastoral. Morris, in describing the book as "a majestic epistle, dealing with grand themes," finds along with other scholars, twelve purposes/occasions for the book, including: (1) A Compendium of Christian Thinking; (4) A Circular Letter; (7) Apostolic Foundation; and (11) A Dialogue with Judaism. The concept of the book being "a dialogue with Judaism" will be of primary importance in this book as it deals particularly with Rom 9:1–5 and chapters 9–11 in general.

38. Osborne, *Romans*, 232; Fitzmyer, *Romans*, 40; Dunn, "Romans, Letter to the," 838; and Shedd, *Commentary on Romans*, 3.

39. Osborne, *Romans*, 40–42.

40. Fitzmyer's speculation can be traced to scholars such as Baur, *Paul*, 352–65.

authorship should be accepted. Therefore, the dating and location for the writing of the epistle by Paul can be assigned to the mid- or late-50s (primarily seen as either AD 55, 56, or 57) from Corinth (see Rom 16:3, including a correlated reference found in 1 Cor 16:19 as it relates to Priscilla and Aquilla).[41]

CONCLUDING THOUGHTS ON THE CHURCH AT ROME

People view Rome with a variety of different adjectives–romantic, grand, old, or historic. For hundreds of years, Rome was the center of the Western world. Today, Rome offers tourists grand photo-ops and historians the chance to tour the crumbling ruins of the Coliseum. Rome is home to decadence and the Pope.

While the prestige of this city on seven hills has dissipated over time, Rome still holds a fascination for the world. For the streets, now filled with tourists, bear witness to the past footsteps of Julius, Caligiula, and Nero. While you can visit the busts and statues of the emperors at museums, the lasting legacy of the city of Rome is the small church planted there, whether by Peter or someone else. This small assembly of believers changed the world. Too often, we forget that the Jewish people were the first people it was to change. Rom 9:1–5 (along with other passages) seeks to remind us of this truth . . . if only we will listen.

---

41. Bell, *Provoked to Jealousy*, 68–69, 78; Morris, *Epistle to the Romans*, 6–7; Osborne, *Romans*, 232; Dunn, "Romans, Letter to the," 838; and Fitzmyer, *Romans*, 86–87.

PART TWO

Introduction to Chapters 3 and 4

After completing "Baby Greek" at Southwestern Baptist Theological Seminary, I looked with trepidation at the fall schedule to see who was teaching New Testament Greek. I admit that I was hoping for the "easy professor," and was intimidated to see the name Siegfried Schatzmann by the Monday night class—the only option for my schedule.

Dr. Schatzmann is a genius in the area of textual criticism, and one can be certain that they will know their Greek after leaving his class. The reputation Dr. Schatzmann has for being difficult is well-earned and well-deserved. He is tough!

However, I walked away from Dr. Schatzmann's class with not only a knowledge of the Greek New Testament, but also a deep appreciation for the shading and nuances one finds in the original language. Seeing the Bible in Greek (and Hebrew as well) opens up doors to understanding and interpretation that are missed if one only reads the Scripture in English. I personally believe that good exegesis is impossible without at least a cursory knowledge of Hebrew and Greek.

Therefore, this next section for examination seeks to provide an exegetical examination of 1 Thess 2:13–16 and Rom 9:1–5. Failure to provide this examination opens the doors to the Thessalonians passage being read as either anti-Semitic or as an interpolation. Without exegetical study, Rom 9:1–5 is open to issues of either dual covenantalism or replacement theology ... or even both, but before we get to those controversies, let us begin the study with exegesis.

3

Exegetical Understanding of 1 Thessalonians 2:13–16

The church at Thessalonica was undergoing persecution when Paul first wrote these two letters. However, Paul knew he could count on them. They were loyal to the Gospel. They were faithful despite the maltreatment they were facing. They believed in the testimony and work of the apostle who brought them the Gospel. Therefore, this brief vignette of the epistle that is before us offers both appreciation for their faithfulness along with comfort and hope for their pain. In addition, we will consider some of the word choices that were interesting then and confounding to this day.

EXPRESSION OF THANKFULNESS FOR THE TESTIMONY OF THE THESSALONIANS (2:13)

> [13]And because of this we give thanks to God constantly, because having received (the) word (by) hearing from our God you did not receive (the) word of men, but as it is actually the word of God which is at work in you who believe.[1]

This section of Paul's letter to the Thessalonian church begins with a καὶ ... καὶ ἡμεῖς construction which can be interpreted as two related but distinct expressions of thanksgiving.[2] First, Paul's expression of appreciation to them for their faithfulness despite their circumstances and, secondly, his thankfulness to God that Paul's work was not done in vain

---

1. Unless otherwise noted, all scripture citations are the translations of the writer.
2. Murrell, "The Human Paul of the New Testament," 174. Murrell believes that this thanksgiving expression was written as a double expression (see 1:2ff.) for either emphasis or to "reconnect the conversation in 1:2–10 with 2:14ff. after the Pauline tangent in 2:1–12."

(3:5).³ The use of the present tense verb εὐχαριστοῦμεν, "we give thanks," also indicates a recurrent theme found in the entire letter (1:2; 3:9; 5:18).⁴ Paul is grateful for their spirit and witness⁵ and he indicates his thankfulness by the use of the adverb, ἀδιαλείπτως, which can be translated as "constantly" as opposed to "without ceasing."⁶

A further question of analysis, in regards to καὶ διὰ τοῦτο καὶ ἡμεῖς ("And because of this we"), is the question of whether Paul is continuing with a declaration of thanksgiving or beginning a new one. The appearance of ὅτι παραλαβόντες ("because having received"⁷) as a temporal adverb expression (aorist active participle) in the next section of the verse, strongly indicates that Paul is looking ahead as he has already devoted a significant portion of the letter to what has been done in and through the Thessalonian church.⁸ Therefore, one can realize that while Paul is writing concerning the past, he is looking forward in anticipation of the future.

The people of the Thessalonian church, as illustrations of people with the gift of spiritual discernment and people who will not fall victim to the falsehoods of men, exemplify what Charles Wanamaker describes as "a source of power in the lives of those who believed."⁹ Ultimately, the Thessalonian church members were able to separate what might have sounded good but offered little eternal value from that which appeared difficult but provided wisdom for the ages.

Abraham Malherbe utilizes the sage Plutarch to clarify the subtle lesson that Paul was attempting to explain in his use of the expression, ἐδέξασθε οὐ,¹⁰ ("you did not receive"). Plutarch once wrote that a wise listener "has the habit of listening with restraint and respect, takes in and

---

3. Frame, *A Critical and Exegetical Commentary on the Epistles of St. Paul to the Thessalonian*, 106; Wanamaker, *The Epistle to the Thessalonians*, 110.

4. Holmes, *1 and 2 Thessalonians*, 80. See also, Hiebert, *The Thessalonian Epistles*, 108.

5. Holmes, *1 and 2 Thessalonians*, 80; Hiebert, *The Thessalonian Epistles*, 108.

6. Hiebert, *The Thessalonian Epistles*, 108.

7. The New American Standard (NASB) translates this expression as "when received."

8. Martin, *1, 2 Thessalonians*, 88–89; Wanamaker, *The Epistle to the Thessalonians*, 110; and Green, *The Letter to the Thessalonians*, 139.

9. Wanamaker, *The Epistle to the Thessalonians*, 111–12.

10. This verb, δέχομαι, is a constative aorist (middle) in the 2nd person plural. Paul's use of a constative aorist indicates that Paul was expressing a fact, not in time or event, but as a reality. See also Wallace, *Greek Grammar*, 557.

Exegetical Understanding of 1 Thessalonians 2:13–16

masters a useful discourse, and more readily sees through and detects a useless or false one."[11] This philosophical concept is something Paul would have experienced during his days as Gamaliel's prodigy (Acts 22:3).[12] Paul utilized and synthesized his Jewish educational background, while striving to equip predominantly Gentile churches with the phrase, ὅτι παραλαβόντες λόγον ἀκοῆς παρ᾽ ἡμῶν τοῦ θεοῦ ἐδέξασθε οὐ λόγον ἀνθρώπων[13] ("because having received [the] word [by] hearing from our God you did not receive [the] word of men").[14] Charles Wanamaker understands the choice of Paul's wording to reflect the concept of not only a reference back to his Jewish educational background but also to the reality that the message being heard by the Thessalonian church was of "divine origin."[15]

The final clause of verse 13, ἀλλὰ καθώς ἐστιν ἀληθῶς λόγον θεοῦ ὃ καὶ ἐνεργεῖται ἐν ὑμῖν τοῖς πιστεύουσιν, ("but as it is actually the word of God which is at work in you who believe") emphasizes the concept of the work of God and the people in whom the work of God is being accomplished. The present middle verb for "work," ἐνεργέω indicates that for the Thessalonians the work is continuing and not something that happened once and was sufficient for the entirety of their Christian lives.[16] In other words, Paul could utilize one of his sports metaphors and tell them they are in a marathon and not a sprint.

An important concept which Paul emphasizes to the Thessalonians is that the work is not about anything that they are doing but the word

---

11. Malherbe, *The Letter to the Thessalonians*, 166. Malherbe specifically uses Plutarch's *On Listening to Lectures* 39C for this comparison and notes that while Plutarch specifically uses a derivative of λαμβάνω, the context and sense remain the same.

12. Schippers, "The Pre-Synoptic Tradition in 1 Thessalonians II 13–16," 229–30; Green, *The Letter to the Thessalonians*, 139; Best, *The First and Second Epistles to the Thessalonians*, 110–12. Schippers draws the allusion to the Jewish style of teaching by stating that ἀκοη "is the Greek equivalent of the rabbinic *shemuah*."

13. In this context, ἀνθρώπων, should be understood as possessive genitive.

14. Best, *The First and Second Epistles to the Thessalonians*, 110.

15. Wanamaker, *The Epistles to the Thessalonians*, 111. See also Williams, *1 and 2 Thessalonians*, 45, 51.

16. Williams, *1 and 2 Thessalonians*, 45; Marshall, *1 and 2 Thessalonians*, 77; and Martin, *1, 2 Thessalonians*, 88. Marshall indicates that the word ἐνεργειται could also be translated in the passive tense as "which is being worked" without a change in exegetical understanding. Marshall could be correct in his assessment; however, the absence of the passive voice provides a truer understanding of the active work of God in the lives of believers.

(λόγον) of God in and through them.[17] The adjectival phrase, ἐν ὑμῖν τοῖς πιστεύουσιν, serves as a present active attributive participle to indicate not simply "to those who believe about Jesus Christ" but "to those who have become believers in Jesus as Messiah."[18] Therefore, the present tense verb of ἐνεργεῖται ["at work"] combined with the present participial phrase ἐν ὑμῖν τοῖς πιστεύουσιν ("in you who believe") reveals that genuine faith is a continuing faith as it is the power of God doing the work in their lives.[19]

GOD'S WORD HAS ENABLED THE THESSALONIANS TO MATURE IN SPITE OF OPPOSITION (2:14–16A)

> [14] For you became imitators, brothers, of the churches of God in Christ which are in Judea, because you suffered the same things also from your own countrymen just as they also from the Jews, [15] the ones who put to death the Lord Jesus and the prophets and severely persecuted us and are not pleasing to God and who are hostile to all men, [16] forbidding us to speak to the Gentiles in order that they might be saved.

Suffering is a theological concept that has become increasingly unpopular in an American Christianity which appears to focus on health and wealth at the expense of sacrifice and poverty. Yet Paul, who would have more common in areas of the today's world in which Christians have to hide and fight and survive for their faith, draws a simple line of reality when he expresses that having the word of God at work in the lives of Christians (see v. 13) requires a sense of both individual and corporate suffering since what they are experiencing is synonymous with the tribulations of the Judean church.[20] Therefore, in one sense we should disagree with Niels Willert who states that Paul was teaching that suffering equated the

---

17. Bruce, *1 & 2 Thessalonians*, 45; Green, *The Letter to the Thessalonians*, 141; and Malherbe, *The Letter to the Thessalonians*, 167.

18. Wallace, *Greek Grammar*, 621. Wallace considers τοι πιστεύουσιν as a substantival adjectival participle that was used to amplify "the soteriological context" of the verse and that the aorist participle in this clause was used to describe a believer as a "live option."

19. Hiebert, *The Thessalonian Epistles*, 111; Milligan, *St. Paul's Epistles to the Thessalonians*, 29.

20. This idea of corporate or joint suffering will be analyzed in greater detail in the following pages of this chapter.

Christian walk.[21] However, a better interpretation would be to see that Paul was providing the promise that they are not alone even in the midst of their suffering.

Ability to Withstand Persecution Common to the Judean Church (v. 14)

Many biblical scholars and commentators are left at a theological quandary as to a proper interpretation to verses 14–16. The simplest answer for many, and as will be discussed in more detail in chapter five, is to see these verses as an interpolation and not reflective of a true Pauline message. However, this answer deflects from Paul's desire both to commend the working and living faith of the Thessalonians as well as to illustrate the depth of depravity which can occur when a person or people group rejects the reality that Jesus is the Messiah. In other words, and recognizing that this truth broke Paul's heart (i.e., Rom 9:1–5), rejecting the truth of Jesus will result in spiritual destruction.

Paul commended the church at Thessalonica for having become imitators (μιμηταὶ) of the Judean church.[22] This concept of imitation should not be seen, as supposed by Willert,[23] as mere mimicking. Rather this imitation that Paul described should be understood as the common cause of Christians, whether in Thessalonica or Judea.[24] In fact, James Moffatt saw this commonality of suffering as Paul's affirmation that they were indeed a member of the "legitimate succession of churches."[25] This concept of succession, while interesting, deflects from the original purpose of Paul's letter to the church, which is that through their suffering they have allowed the word of God[26] to be at work in them (see v. 13).

---

21. Willert, "Catalogues of Hardships in the Pauline Correspondence," 230.

22. The Greek word for church (ἐκκλησιῶν) is used in this role as an attributive genitive. The overall concept for churches is that the churches belong to God (τοῦ Θεοῦ) and not the members in attendance.

23. Willert, "Catalogues of Hardships in the Pauline Correspondence," 229.

24. Wanamaker, *The Epistles to the Thessalonians*, 112; Marshall, *1 and 2 Thessalonians*, 78; Bruce, *1 & 2 Thessalonians*, 45; Taylor, "Who Persecuted the Thessalonian Christians?," 788; and Best, *The First and Second Epistles to the Thessalonians*, 113. Taylor did not see imitation in the English connotation of the word but rather "that Paul is making a comparison between the endurance of the Judaean Christians in the face of harassment from their compatriots and that of the Thessalonians."

25. Moffatt, *The First and Second Epistles to the Thessalonians*, 29.

26. Θεοῦ is used here in the role of a possessive genitive.

The concept of suffering is not new. From the story of Job to the reality of the cross, suffering is found throughout Scripture. Therefore, Paul's mention of suffering was not a surprising concept for the Thessalonian church. N. H. Taylor states that the Thessalonian church is the first church recognized in Scripture as a victim of persecution.[27] What was new, however, was the thought that suffering could be a unifying theme for the first-century Christian world.[28]

The aorist active word for "suffering,"[29] ἐπάθετε, gives the sense that they had already suffered at the hands of their own people (ὑπὸ τῶν ἰδίων συμφυλετῶν). The phrase, "your own countrymen," offers one of the keys to a proper exposition of the passage. Many commentators view the root word, συμφυλετής, as referring to a people group or as a "synonym for Gentiles."[30] Other commentators choose to include the Thessalonian Jews as members of συμφυλετής[31] despite the fact that the Attic Greek meaning of the word is "one belonging to the same tribe."[32]

To include the Thessalonian Jews as members of the συμφυλετής is to force a translation that would prove the accusations of a polemical attack. However, Paul is instead comparing the Thessalonian church to the church in Judea by drawing the parallel that opponents of the Gospel are everywhere and within every people group. Gentiles and Jews alike who

---

27. Taylor, "Who Persecuted the Thessalonian Christians?" 784.

28. Dodd, *The Problem with Paul* 119. See also Martin, *1, 2 Thessalonians*, 89.

29. Best, *The First and Second Epistles to the Thessalonians*, 116, incorrectly ascribes the suffering mentioned in verse 15 to Paul and his companions due to the fact that the verb is in the past tense. To interpret it as a strictly Pauline suffering not only diminishes but also circumnavigates the suffering experienced by the Thessalonian church, as this is the point of the passage.

30. Patte, "Anti-Semitism in the New Testament. Confronting the Dark Side of Paul's and Matthew's Teaching," 46; Martin, *1, 2 Thessalonians*, 89; Green, *The Letters to the Thessalonians*, 142; Frame, *A Critical and Exegetical Commentary on the Epistles of St. Paul to the Thessalonians*, 110; Taylor, "Who Persecuted the Thessalonian Christians?" 793; and Bruce, *1 & 2 Thessalonians*, 46.

31. Taylor, "Who Persecuted the Thessalonian Christians?" 793; Donfried, *Paul, Thessalonica, and Early Christianity*, 128.

32. Riesner, *Paul's Early Period*, 352; Donfried, *Paul, Thessalonica, and Early Christianity*, 128; and Balz, H. "συμφυλέτης." In *Exegetical Dictionary of the New Testament* (*EDNT*). See also Milligan *St. Paul's Epistles to the Thessalonians*, 29), who while agreeing with Bruce's translation, *1 & 2 Thessalonians*, of συμφυλετής (46) as "being from the same tribe," still chooses to include the Thessalonian Jews as potential instigators of the persecution.

reject the message of Messiah Jesus will oppose the witness of those who believe in Him, even at the cost of Jewish and Gentile Christian lives.[33]

When examining τῶν Ἰουδαίων, "of the Jews," Gerhard Kittel[34] does not limit his analysis of the word/phrase, "ὁ Ἰουδαῖος," to simply this one word but looks at the entire language canvas to develop an overall concept of the expression.[35] The primary use of the term, Ἰουδαῖος, was not the traditional use for a member of the Jewish nation until after the fall of the Northern Kingdom in 722 BC. The term then changed from strictly a nationalistic sense to a more religious confessional description.[36]

The original term, Ἰσραήλ, can be seen as both a personal and tribal name, according to Mayer,[37] or as a "sacral league of tribes" who were established as a nation in Joshua 24.[38] A strictly religious understanding of Ἰσραήλ is viewed through the covenantal lenses of God's promise to Abraham.[39]

The negative connotation of the term τῶν Ἰουδαίων came to prominence primarily during the time of Christ.[40] Paul himself utilized the term not in derision but in classifying himself as a Jew of the Jews (Rom 11:1).[41] He also used it as a means of separation between Jews and Greeks (Rom 1:16; 2:9–10).[42] Therefore one could assume that if Paul chose to differentiate between people groups, he could also use a nationalistic term to

33. Milligan, *St. Paul's Epistles to the Thessalonians*, 30; Donfried, *Paul, Thessalonica, and Early Christianity*, 95; and Still, *Conflict at Thessalonica*, 130–31.

34. It would be irresponsible to utilize Kittel's *Theological Dictionary of the New Testament* without providing a brief acknowledgement of his anti-Semitic views. Kittel was a member of the Nazi Party both before and during the Second World War. In a post-war Europe, Kittel was arrested, imprisoned, and ostracized for his anti-Semitic points of views (Ericksen, *Theologians Under Hitler*, 28–78; Gerdmar, *Roots of Theological Anti-Semitism*, 417–530).

35. Kittel, ed., *Theological Dictionary of the New Testament (TDNT)*, 356. Kittel allows the writers (von Rad, K. G. Kuhn, and Gutbrod) of these sections to include the words, "Ἰσραήλ, Ἰσραηλίτης, Ἰουδαῖος, Ἰουδαία, Ἰουδαϊκός, ἰουδαΐζω, Ἰουδαϊσμός, Ἑβραῖος, Ἑβραϊκός, ἑβραΐς, ἑβραϊστί," as synonymous for the concept of "Jew."

36. Kittel, *TDNT*, 359. See also, *EDNT*, II, 192; and Mayer, "Ἰσραήλ." In *The New International Dictionary of New Testament Theology (NIDNTT)*, 310.

37. Mayer, *NIDNTT*, 304–5.

38. *TDNT*, III, 356–57.

39. Campbell, "Israel," in *Dictionary of Paul and His Letters*, 441.

40. Mayer, *NIDNTT*, 311.

41. Frame, *A Critical and Exegetical Commentary on the Epistles of St. Paul*, 110.

42. *EDNT*: II, 195.

differentiate between believers and non-believers within the same group.[43] A further observation regarding τῶν' Ἰουδαίων is that as a Jew, Paul was accustomed to using a description which "reflects the polemical idiom of an in-house debate."[44]

Another crucial phrasing issue is the wording "who killed the Lord Jesus" in verse 15 (τῶν καὶ τὸν κύριον ἀποκτεινάντων Ἰησοῦν). This phrasing separates the traditional form of "Lord Jesus" by using the "killed" participle of ἀποκτείνω. This separation is designed to highlight and centralize that it was indeed Jesus who was killed by "the Jews."[45] This phrasing is an unusual way of describing the death of the Lord. However, it is not cause for concern or an examination worthy of a textual variance.

The UBS (4th ed.) text instead notes that there are textual disagreements as it pertains to the word προφήτα (accusative direct object).[46] For even while this usage receives an "A" rating, an alternate translation is listed as ἰδίους προφήτας which would be translated as "their own prophets." This alternate translation does not provide a substantial difference in interpretation except to center the focus, or eliminate all doubt, on the idea that Paul is writing about the death of the Jewish prophets from the Old Testament.[47] Either translation is an acceptable reading; however, this could present a problem in the exposition if one believes that Paul was projecting himself into the prophet role via the phrase "and drove us out" (καὶ ἡμᾶς ἐκδιωξάντων).[48]

The Jewish "Punishment" for Their Unbelief–God's Disappointment (v.15b–16a)

The five accusations against the "the Jews" in verses 15b and 16a have been separated so as to amplify the perpetual cycle of sin which had been at-

---

43. *TDNT*: III, 380; Martin, *1, 2 Thessalonians*, 90–91.

44. Hagner, "Paul's Quarrel with Judaism," 134. See also, Dodd, *The Problem with Paul*, 119–20; Holmes, *1 and 2 Thessalonians*, 86–87; Wanamaker, *The Epistles to the Thessalonians*, 118; and Holtz, "The Judgment on the Jews and the Salvation of All Israel," 285, 286.

45. Williams, *1 and 2 Thessalonians*, 47; Hiebert, *The Thessalonian Epistles*, 115; and Gilliard, "Paul and the Killing of the Prophets," 266.

46. *The Greek New Testament* (UBS), 700.

47. Weatherly, "The Authenticity of 2.13–16," 87; and Hiebert, *The Thessalonian Epistles*, 116.

48. Tellbe, *Paul between Synagogue and State*, 109.

tributed to "the Jews." Their "sin" began with the death of the Lord Jesus and included murdering and persecuting other religious (Messianic) opponents. This sin of persecution created within them a desire to forbid others from hearing about the Gospel message, thus returning them to their "sin" which began with the death of Messiah Jesus.[49] However, before, we become too presumptuous about "the Jews", let us also remember that the same sin would have been held against us before our own salvation.

One issue which has been raised, not necessarily as an argument for interpolation (see chapter five), is the joint concept of being displeasing to God and demonstrating hostility to humanity (καὶ θεῷ μὴ ἀρεσκόντων καὶ πᾶσιν ἀνθρώποις ἐναντίων).[50] F. F. Bruce considers this to be a piece of "indiscriminate anti-Jewish polemic."[51] Gene Green, however, sees this expression as a continuation of Old Testament themes (Num 23:27; 1 Kgs 3:10; Ps 69:31).[52] Ernest Best agrees with Green because he links this hostility to the Jewish fear of losing their place as the "privileged people of God."[53] Consequently, it should be understood that hostility towards those who proclaim the truth of Jesus is actually hostility towards God and his plan for the nations.[54]

Verse 16 begins with the present active participial clause, "forbidding us to speak to the Gentiles in order that they might be saved." This is an intriguing statement which begs the question of why did the Jewish leaders deem it necessary to attempt to prevent the message of Jesus from

---

49. Best, *The First and Second Epistles to the Thessalonians*, 116; Hiebert, *The Thessalonian Epistle*, 115. Still, *Conflict at Thessalonica*, (p. 133–35) accurately perceives ἐκδιωξάντων to be an aorist participle. This does not necessarily change the meaning of the verb but does allow for alternate interpretations, including Still's view that Paul is referring to his immediate past banishment from Thessalonica. The conclusion of this writer, in agreement with Still, is that the phrase "severely persecuted" should be seen in light of the fact that the actions of the past are ever constant and are evidenced by present deeds. In other words, the cycle continues.

50. Bockmuehl, "1 Thessalonians 2:14–16 and the Church in Jerusalem," 14, 15; and Bruce, *1 & 2 Thessalonians*, 47. One should also note that θεω and ἀνθρώποι are utilized in this sentence as datives of direct object.

51. Bruce, *1 & 2 Thessalonians*, 47.

52. Green, *The Letters to the Thessalonians*, 145–46. Green also rejects Bruce's argument of anti-Jewish polemic by stressing that Paul "limits the critique to Jewish opposition to God's mission."

53. Best, *The First and Second Epistles to the Thessalonians*, 117–18.

54. Marshall, *1 and 2 Thessalonians*, 79; Frame, *A Critical and Exegetical Commentary on the Epistles of St. Paul to the Thessalonians*, 112; Still, *Conflict at Thessalonica*, 136; Milligan, *St. Paul's Epistles to the Thessalonians*, 31; and Hiebert, *The Thessalonian Epistles*, 117–18.

being spread to the Gentiles? The rationale of the Jewish leaders is not easily explained, except to say that their anger against the teachings of Jesus, and consequently Paul, extended to not wanting the message to be heard by anyone. Any attempt to answering the question of "why" that goes beyond scripture and into the area of psychoanalysis is something we must avoid because it often leads to assumption rather than truth.

In utilizing scripture, Paul emphasizes this reality of prevention by the use of the active participle of κωλύω. This "forbidding" was connected to the aorist infinitive λαλῆσαι. Wanamaker viewed this phrase as not simply connected to the phrases of verse 15 but more importantly as an explanation for the phrase "who are hostile to all men."[55] This hostility against the Gentiles hearing the message of Jesus of Nazareth led to Paul's use of σωθῶιν ("saved") in conjunction with the ἵνα ("in order that") purpose clause.[56] Paul's focus was on the salvation of the Gentiles whereas the focus of the Jewish leaders in verses 14 and 15 was to stop the message from being heard by anyone.

JUDGMENT UPON "THE JEWS" FOR THEIR ACTIONS (2:16B)

> [16] with the result that they always fill up the measure of their sins. But wrath has come upon them to the utmost.

The final section of the passage in question is for many biblical scholars the most troubling, especially for those commentators who reject the concept of interpolation (see chapter five for a detailed consideration of this controversy).

> St. Paul's intemperate outburst against "the Jews" in 1 Thessalonians 2:14–16 has long troubled the politically reconstructed, post-Holocaust guild of *Neutestamentler*. How can the same man possibly have believed that God's wrath and definitive condemnation have "finally come upon" the Jews—only to claim elsewhere that "all Israel will be saved"?[57]

---

55. Wanamaker, *The Epistles to the Thessalonians*, 15. See also Williams, *1 and 2 Thessalonians*, 48.

56. Wanamaker, *The Epistles to the Thessalonians*, 116.

57. Bockmuehl, "1 Thessalonians 2:14–16 and the Church in Jerusalem," 1.

Exegetical Understanding of 1 Thessalonians 2:13–16

The root of Bockmuehl's question, however, does not lie in whether Paul meant what he said in 1 Thess 2:16[58] but whether it can be accepted that the statement is not in contradiction to other Pauline passages, specifically Romans 9–11 (specifically 9:1–5).[59] If one chooses to view the verse as simply representative of Paul's commitment to evangelism,[60] one limits a complete understanding of the passage. The proper choice to make then is to examine how seemingly contradictory passages are in fact complementary of each other.[61]

To Fill Up the Measure of Their Sins[62]

The infinitive expression,[63] εἰς τὸ ἀναπληρῶσαι αὐτῶν τὰς ἁμαρτίας πάντοτε, brings to mind the idea that "the Jews" are guilty of incurring God's wrath since the time of the prophets or even earlier.[64] This view is given additional credence when one examines the root verb, ἀναπληρόω, and discovers that it should be recognized within the eschatological framework as something that has already happened.[65] The adverb, πάν-

---

58. Bockmuehl, "1 Thessalonians 2:14–16 and the Church in Jerusalem," 1.

59. Wanamaker, *The Epistles to the Thessalonians*, 118; Taylor, "Who Persecuted the Thessalonian Christians?" 788.

60. Schreiner, *Paul: Apostle of God's Glory in Christ*, 473.

61. The reconciliation of the passages in question will be conducted at the conclusion of chapters five through seven and in the conclusion.

62. Many biblical scholars have commented on the similarity of this passage to the pseudepigraphical *Testament of Levi 6:11*. This paper will not focus on the similarities but wanted to note that such a conversation exists in scholarly circles. Two examples of the scholarly examination of the impact that the *Testament of Levi 6:11* might have had on Paul are Lamp, "Is Paul Anti-Jewish?: *Testament of Levi 6* in the Interpretation of 1 Thessalonians 2:13–16," 408–27; and Baarda, "The Shechem Episode in the Testament of Levi," 11–73.

63. Wanamaker, *The Epistles to the Thessalonians*, 116. Wanamaker views the use of the expression εἰς τὸ as one of purpose to illustrate that the sins of the Jewish leaders was purposeful and is found in parallel expression in Romans 11 (11:7–10, 28, 32).

64. Steele, "Jewish Scriptures in 1 Thessalonians," 13; Wanamaker, *The Epistles to the Thessalonians*, 116; Marshall, *1 and 2 Thessalonians*, 80; Green, *The Letters to the Thessalonians*, 147; and Bockmuehl, "1 Thessalonians 2:14–16 and the Church in Jerusalem," 9. See also, Forestell, "The Letters to the Thessalonians (1 Thess)," 230.

65. Hagner, "Paul's Quarrel with Judaism," 132–33; and Steele, "Jewish Scriptures in 1 Thessalonians," 13.

τοτε, however, presents problems because of its forward-looking sense of history.⁶⁶ Therefore, alternate viewpoints should be considered.

I. Howard Marshall and D. Edmond Hiebert, using the analogies of a cup or measuring scale, prefer to view this section as referring to something that is even now occurring until the full measure is revealed at the end.⁶⁷ Wanamaker concurs with the cup or measure analogy and links it to Jesus' final condemnation of the Pharisees in Matt 23. This is an interesting connecting point in light of the fact that Paul as a Pharisee, in his pre-conversion days, would have been one of the condemned at the time of Jesus' message.⁶⁸ Therefore, the Thessalonian church can see the promise and hope that forgiveness is still possible even for those who are filling up the measure of their sins.

The Reality of the Coming Wrath

In the final portion of verse 16, ἔφθασεν δὲ ἐπ᾽ αὐτοὺς ἡ ὀργὴ εἰ τέλος, the concept of "wrath" (ὀργὴ⁶⁹) is key to a proper exegesis and understanding of this passage. The wrath (ὀργὴ) of God is something that no one should take lightly, whether it be in the figurative or literal sense. Therefore, the wrath mentioned in verse 16b should be considered as a separate unit in this section of the chapter. The verb "has come" (ἔφθασεν) and the prepositional phrase (εἰς τέλος) will receive individual attention as well.

---

66. Best, *The First and Second Epistles to the Thessalonians*, 118; Wanamaker, *The Epistles to the Thessalonians*, 116; and Marshall, *1 and 2 Thessalonians*, 80. Best explains the confusion regarding the word choices as a time in which the "definite measure of sins" will be completed and "be followed by God's judgment." In other words, the measure of sins has been filled in an eschatological sense, but is simply waiting for temporal reality to *catch up* with the reality of the eschaton.

67. Wallace, *Greek Grammar*, 563–64; Marshall, *1 and 2 Thessalonians*, 80; and Hiebert, *The Thessalonian Epistles*, 119. Wallace sees this as a potential example of the proleptic aorist. An aorist that describes an event still to be culminated even though it is described as already completed. Wallace stresses that this type of aorist is used "to stress the certainty of the event" (564).

68. Wanamaker, *The Epistles to the Thessalonians*, 116–17; and Donfried, "Paul and Judaism," 249.

69. Bauer, "ὀργή, ης, ἡ." *A Greek-English Lexicon of the New Testament and Other Early Christian Literature*, 582–83. The lexicon speaks specifically of ὀργή as being representative of the wrath of God. A "wrath" that is different than anger or indignation because of His need to pass judgment upon the people ("the Jews"). Bauer separates this particular usage from future judgment and gives it the sense of past and/or present judgment.

The wrath mentioned in 2:16b should not be regarded as simple anger but as a wrath resulting in judgment. The question to be answered then is whether the wrath is current or eschatological in nature. If one chooses to view wrath in an eschatological sense, the use of "wrath" in 1:10 with the participle ἐρχομένη (which is coming) lends textual and contextual support.[70] In order to support the view of wrath as a present reality, one must find historical evidence of judgment occurring or having occurred. Birger Pearson views the fall of Jerusalem in AD 70 as an event which provides sufficient destructive magnitude.[71] Todd Still prefers to date the expulsion of Jews from Rome in AD 49 or the massacre of Jews in Jerusalem in AD 50 as more likely events to describe "the wrath" that Paul mentions in 1 Thessalonians.[72] Markus Bockmuehl centers his focus on the early to mid-40s as a possible date for the wrath due to the fact that Jerusalem was going through the famine mentioned by Paul (Rom 15:26; cf. Acts 11:27–30) and violent upheavals during the rule of Ventidius Cumanus.[73]

The evidence, however, tends to support the view of a future, or eschatological wrath, which raises a second question–who is destined to be the victims of the wrath described in this verse? If one believes that Paul is expressing an anti-Semitic viewpoint,[74] then all Jews and not only "the Jews" mentioned in the passage are destined for perdition. If one believes that Paul was referring to only those Jews who reject the gift of salvation, then there remains hope and the possibility of eternal life as amplified in Rom 11:26.[75]

---

70. Wanamaker, *The Epistles to the Thessalonians*, 117; Bruce, *1 & 2 Thessalonians*, 48; and Donfried, "Paul and Judaism," 252–53.

71. Pearson, "1 Thessalonians 2:13–16," 83.

72. Still, *Conflict at Thessalonica*, 35–36; Taylor, "Who Persecuted the Thessalonian Christians?"786; and Forestell, "The Letter to the Thessalonians (1 Thes)," 230.

73. Bockmuehl, "1 Thessalonians 2:14–16 and the Church in Jerusalem," 30. For additional information on the reign of Cumanus and the tumult in Jerusalem and Samaria during his period of rule, see M. Aberbach, "The Conflicting Accounts of Josephus and Tacitus Concerning Cumanus' and Felix' Terms of Office," 1–14.

74. Best, *The First and Second Epistles to the Thessalonians*, 122.

75. Schreiner, *Paul*, 474; and Marshall, *1 and 2 Thessalonians*, 83. Marshall, in expressing this view, wrote:

> The prophecy that all Israel will be saved means that Paul expected a different response from the Jews than was presently the case, but does not exclude the need for their faith in Jesus Christ in order to be saved; nor obviously does it

A further examination requires one to examine the aorist verb form, ἔφθασεν from φθάνω, meaning "has come." The preferred explanation of this book is to see this aorist form as a proleptic aorist because it provides one with the sense that the wrath is present but still to come in the eschatological sense of the word.[76]

In concluding the exegesis of 1 Thess 2:13–16, one comes to the phrase, εἰς τέλος, which is translated in the NASB as "to the utmost," giving the sense that the wrath of God upon the Jews is irreversible.[77] The difficulty can be avoided not on the basis of how εἰς τέλος[78] is translated but in recognizing that this is referring to "the Jews" who have rejected the Messiah.[79] It is exegetically improper to tarnish an entire people group with eternal damnation because of the actions of a few.[80] However, it would be equally improper to assume that all of the Jewish people are guaranteed a place in the kingdom simply because they are Jews.[81] I. Howard Marshall succinctly explains that the choice for an eternity with Christ or an eternity without Him is individual and not nationalistic.[82]

---

mean that individual Israelites may not be converted during the present time. The man who wrote Rom 9:1–5; 10:1 is hardly likely to have been guilty of anti-Semitism at any time.

76. Williams, *1 and 2 Thessalonians*, 49; Beker, *The Triumph of God*, 82; and Frame, *A Critical and Exegetical Commentary on the Epistles of St. Paul to the Thessalonians*, 114. The alternate view "has already come" is supported by both interpolation advocates and opponents. See Okeke, "I Thessalonians 2.13–16," 130; and Green, *The Letters to the Thessalonians*, 149. However, this view negates and ignores the importance of developing an interpretation compatible to Romans 9–11, and specifically the other passage in question in this book.

77. Ellis, *Paul's Use of the Old Testament*, 77, 154. Page citations are to the reprint edition. Ellis notes that Paul's word choice, "to the utmost," is actually a Jewish idiom. Therefore, it is the view of this writer that any and all Jewish people who read the epistle would understand the concept which Paul was attempting to express. Ellis also provides a reader with both an Old Testament example(s) of this idiom (Gen 15:16; Ps 78:6) and an apocryphal illustration (2 Macc 6:14).

78. τέλος in this position serves as an accusative after the preposition εἰς. The importance of this placement, in the view of the thesis writer, is that one should interpret this section of Scripture not by focusing on "to the utmost" but rather that the wrath of God has come upon the Jewish people. This focus does not detract from the extent of the wrath but rather the trepidation one should fear when the idea of God's wrath is brought into the equation, on whatever level it is introduced.

79. Murrell, "The Human Paul of the New Testament," 175, 176.

80. Green, *The Letters to the Thessalonians*, 94–95; Holtz, "The Judgment on the Jews and the Salvation of All Israel," 284, 286–87; and Wanamaker, *The Epistles to the Thessalonians*, 118.

81. Simpson, "The Problems Posed by 1 Thessalonians," 43.

82. Marshall, *1 and 2 Thessalonians*, 83.

4

Exegetical Understanding of Romans 9:1–5

PAUL DISPLAYED IN SCRIPTURE a wide range of emotions with regard to the Jewish people. In the Thessalonian passage, Paul identifies the Jewish people as murderers of Christ and the prophets. However, in Romans 9:1–5, Paul seems to express an almost inexpressible grief for the spiritual condition of his ethnic brothers and sisters. This wide range of expressions,[1] along with what Garrett sees as the wide-ranging hermeneutical explanations for the entirety of the Romans 9–11 section and the horrifying events of the twentieth century (i.e., the Holocaust),[2] creates the need for an adequate exegetical explanation of the passage. The question must not be simply asked, but also answered regarding just what exactly Paul was saying when he seemed to wish upon himself a sentence of perdition if it would mean the salvation of the Jewish people (Rom 9:3).

For example, theologians, such as Karl Barth, would say that to read the actual Jewish people into this passage would be a mistake, as the Church has replaced Israel as God's chosen people.[3] John MacArthur

---

1. Jewett, "Law and Coexistence," 343. This dichotomy of expressions causes many theologians to grasp for explanations regarding Paul's attitudes toward himself as a Jew and the Jewish people in general. Robert Jewett explores this confusion, as he compares the passage in question to the accusations of anti-Judaism made by such biblical scholars as Rosemary Radford Ruether. See Ruether, *Faith and Fratricide*, 104.

2. Garrett, *Systematic Theology*, 2:440.

3. Barth, *Epistle to the Romans*, 332, 334–35, 337. Barth (332) writes, "And now, in contrast with the Gospel of Jesus Christ, there is thrust upon our attention–Israel, the Church, the world of religion as it appears in history, and we hasten to add, Israel in its purest, truest, and most powerful aspect." See also, Hall, *Christian Anti-Semitism*, 116. Hall cites Augustine as an illustration of how the concept of replacement theology came to the forefront, for Augustine compared the Jewish people to Witness People (as opposed to Chosen people) who were doomed to be witnesses of what happens when one rejects Jesus, and that they are nothing more than "Christ-killers." See Augustine, "Reply to Faustus, the Manichean," 28–32.

would not consider this passage to be a proof-text for replacement theology, but would see it as evidence that the Jewish people have been "temporarily set aside by God," set aside by God so that He could accomplish His divine plan for humanity.[4] J. Christiaan Beker, who holds to a dual covenantal theology, would view this passage, as well as the entirety of chapters 9–11, as evidence of God's confirmation that "the eschatological destiny of Israel" would be evidenced "at the time of the eschatological triumph of God."[5]

Conservative theologians struggle with this issue of how God will keep His promise of "chosenness" to the Jewish people, but at the same time allow many Jews to suffer eternal separation from Him. The primary difference in interpretation, however, is found in the theological conservatives' attempt to see the wonder of God's redemption for any and all in the midst of perdition for the many.[6] Paul himself apparently struggled with this reality as well, as evidenced by the passage in question. He never surrendered the hope and prayer that the Jewish people would come to faith one day, even while lamenting their "lostness." In fact, he began many missionary endeavors in the synagogues, where a Jewish population was present (Acts 13:14–48; 14:1; 17:1–4, 10–12; 18:4–11; 19:8–10, 17; 20:21).[7]

Therefore, the purpose of this exegetical analysis of Romans 9:1–5 will be to probe the context of the passage in relationship to all the book of Romans and, specifically, to chapters 9–11. Additionally, this chapter will examine in detail the meaning of Paul's willingness to go to hell for the Jewish people in light of the idea found in Romans 8 that nothing can separate us from the love of God (8:31–39).[8]

---

4. MacArthur, *Romans 9–16*, 6.

5. Beker, "Romans 9–11," 45.

6. Dodd, *Problem with Paul*, 136; Wakefield, "Romans 9–11," 68; Kaylor, *Paul's Covenant Community*, 186; and Cook, "Christian Witness to the Jews," 147–48.

7. Cook, "Christian Witness to the Jews," 146; and Garrett, *Systematic Theology*, 2:493–94.

8. The issues touched upon in this introductory section of chapter 4 will be examined in further detail in chapters 5–7 of the book.

PAUL'S LAMENT IDENTIFIES THE BREADTH OF HIS LOVE FOR HIS OWN PEOPLE (9:1-2)

¹ I tell (you) the truth in Christ, I do not lie, my own conscience testifying in the Holy Spirit, ² because I have great sorrow and constant distress (in) my heart.

Paul begins chapter 9 by detailing the prospect and promise of the Jewish people with an oath, a testimony, and an examination of his soul,[9] while at the same time analyzing the spiritual and eternal condition of the Jewish people. The tragic destiny of the Jewish people who have rejected Christ is not disguised, but brought to the forefront in the opening verses of chapter 9. By a deliberate stance of honesty, Paul has indicated the eternal state for which the Jewish people are heading; and yet, he continues to hold out a glimmer hope that they will come to receive Messiah Jesus before it is too late.[10]

Therefore, verse 1 opens as a new thought and with no connecting word to the previous chapter. Chapter 8 closed with the glorious reality that nothing can separate us, as Christians, from the love of God,[11] while chapter 9 begins with a lament regarding eternal damnation. This abrupt change of tone has been called a pause,[12] or a point of "solemn emphasis."[13] The solemnity in this passage is made especially poignant by Paul's use of the words, "ἐν Χριστῷ (in Christ)."

In noting the solemnity of ἐν Χριστῷ, Charles Hodge sees three possible interpretations: (1) it is part of an oath formula, (2) it is connected to Paul's relationship with Jesus, or (3) it is evidence of the Christian relationship that we as believers can all have in Christ.[14] Any of the

---

9. Williamson, *Guest in the House of Israel*, 101. While one would, and should, disagree with Williamson's advocacy of Dual Covenant theology, one can agree in principle with his statement that Paul begins this chapter with "a highly emphatic, triple assertion that he is telling the truth, ..."

10. Fraikin, "Rhetorical Function," 101-2.

11. Dunn, *Romans 9-16*, 522; Cranford, "Election and Ethnicity," 29; Bell, *Provoked to Jealousy*, 172; and Sanday and Headlam, *Epistle to the Romans*, 226.

12. Sanday and Headlam, *Epistle to the Romans*, 226; and Dunn, *Romans 9-16*, 522.

13. Cranford, "Election and Ethnicity," 29.

14. Hodge, *Epistle to the Romans*, 294-95. In relation to the first and second option, see also, Osborne, *Romans*, 236. A fourth option is that Paul was not proclaiming an oath, but rather making an assertion which was beyond denial. Plumer, *Commentary on Romans*, 454.

options would be appropriate; however, the first option appears to define most clearly the level of grief of Paul's soul.

The idea of Paul declaring an oath illustrates the level, and maintains the tone to which Paul is willing to go (see v. 3) for the salvation of the Jewish people. The first option stays consistent with the Jewish tradition, as found in Old Testament Scripture and pseudepigraphical literature (Exod 32:30–32; 4 Ezra 8:15–18, 10:6–8, 21–22; 2 Baruch 35:3). Paul would have been extremely familiar with the option of this view.[15] In addition, the oath formula allowed Paul to develop a rhetorical argument that could not be used against him by the Jewish people who opposed the message of Messiah Jesus.[16] Finally, the pledging of an oath drew the Jewish people to the memory of how Moses (Exod 32:31–32) was once willing to be "damned" for the sake of the Jewish people.[17]

Paul's Oath Statement is Proven Through Spiritual Connotations

Paul begins his oath statement with "in Christ" as a declaration that he is speaking the truth, Ἀλήθειαν λέγω. The interesting twist to the sentence, and one which could cause some to place the emphasis of ἐν Χριστῷ on the concept of truth rather than the speaker, is that "ἀλήθειαν ([the] truth)" is found as the first word in the sentence.[18] However, the focus should not be on the direct object of the sentence, but on the subject of the expression.[19]

"The truth," in the sense that Paul is emphasizing the content of his message,[20] is only true because the speaker is in Christ.[21] Daniel Wallace

---

15. Bell, *Provoked to Jealousy*, 172.

16. Cranford, "Election and Ethnicity," 29.

17. Munck, *Christ and Israel*, 29–30. Munck reminds the reader of this parallel by identifying Paul as a *Heilgeschichte* figure—a figure who is prepared to offer himself as a substitute for the people. See also, Guerra, "Romans," 228.

18. Kim, *God, Israel, and the Gentiles*, 100; Moo, *Epistle to the Romans*, 556; and Witherington and Hyatt, *Paul's Letter to the Romans*, 249.

19. Schreiner, *Romans*, 478; and Kim, *God, Israel, and the Gentiles*, 100. Johann Kim notes that Paul should be the focus of the text, not because he is defending himself, but because he feels the need to defend God.

20. Moo, *Epistle to the Romans*, 556; and Witherington and Hyatt, *Paul's Letter to the Romans*, 249.

21. Cranfield, *Epistle to the Romans*, 451–52; Kim, *God, Israel, and the Gentiles*, 99; Jowett, *Epistles of St. Paul*, and Johnson, *Reading Romans*, 154. Johnson notes that the accusation against Paul that he is "a renegade to his own people" places emphasis on why Paul would state so categorically that he is telling the truth.

Exegetical Understanding of Romans 9:1–5

focuses on the speaker by considering the "I tell (you)," expression, "λέγω," as a progressive declaration present instead of a customary present. The verb involves a continuous action instead of merely a repeated action.[22]

The "in Christ" expression emphasizes the reality that, not only does Paul speak the truth, but also that he does not lie, οὐ ψεύδομαι.[23] In addition, Wallace would consider this verb as progressive present, because Paul is not now lying, nor would he be lying in the future.[24] This phrase should not be considered as a parenthetic statement[25] or a simple parallel to "my own conscience testifying in the Holy Spirit."[26] Instead, it should be seen as Paul's manner of speaking in what Calvin described as speaking "without fiction or disguise."[27]

The phrase is its own separate statement and provides proof that Paul is sincere in what he will proclaim in verse 3. Through both phrases, he is "covering the gamut" in his oath-form expressions[28] by emphasizing his honesty and inability to fabricate his emotions or pain. A child-like modern-day equivalent would be as if Paul was telling his readers that "he was swearing on a stack of Bibles AND pinky-swearing."

Consequently, and because Paul "tells the truth" and "does not lie," the Holy Spirit is able to give testimony of Paul's conscience. Wallace does not define the adverbial participle, "συμμαρτυρούσῃ," as another progressive present. However, one should assume that Paul would maintain consistency in his expressions, and so the exegete can be comfortable in stating that this phrase is a progressive present as well.

Joseph Fitzmyer considers this as a parenthetic statement to the opening phrase of the verse.[29] This implied sense of Paul's statement

---

22. Wallace, *Greek Grammar*, 518–19.

23. Denney, *St. Paul's Epistle to the Romans*, 656.

24. Wallace, *Greek Grammar*, 518–19.

25. Fitzmyer, *Romans*, 543. Fitzmyer views this phrase as Paul's method of using negation to formulate his affirmative statement (i.e., 2 Cor 11:31).

26. Liddon, *Explanatory Analysis*, 148; Johnson, *Reading Romans*, 154; Moo, *Epistle to the Romans*, 556; and Kim, *God, Israel, and the Gentiles*, 100.

27. Calvin, *Epistle of Paul the Apostle to the Romans*, 334.

28. Dunn, *Romans 9–16*, 523; and Schreiner, *Romans*, 478-79. Additionally, Schreiner sees this double expression as an apologetic for when he encounters libelous statements from the enemies to the Gospel (i.e., 2 Cor 11:31; Gal 1:20; 1 Tim 2:7).

29. Fitzmyer, *Romans*, 543. Hodge, *Epistle to the Romans*, 295, does not view the phrase as a parenthetic statement, but does believe that the statement should be considered as separate from ἀλήθειαν λέγω and οὐ ψεύδομαι. This writer disagrees with Hodge,

being only a parenthetical insert, as propagated by Fitzmyer,[30] lends itself to an incorrect understanding that the oath statement is not crucial to an understanding of the verse. The correct understanding of the oath statement should be to recognize that each phrase is both building upon the previous statement and magnifying the enormity of what Paul is willing to sacrifice. However, this should not be seen, as MacArthur suggests, as "summoning such an array of witnesses,"[31] for Paul is not calling on the testimony of mere witnesses, but rather the infallible testimony of Jesus and the Holy Spirit.[32] This testimony will then support the rest of the passage, which "begins" in verse 3 with Paul's expression of sorrow.

Paul's Oath Statement is Proven by Physical/Emotional Reactions

The premise established by Paul in verse 1 lays the groundwork for his expressions of how deep his emotions run. This foundation he accomplishes in verse 2 by the use of two nouns serving in the predicate position (λύπη and ὀδύνη)[33] and the verb εἰμί (μοί ἐστιν), which should be considered as a part of a ὅτι επ exegetical clause, because it "explains or clarifies"[34] what is begun in verse 1.

Paul identifies with two physical/emotional states, due to the ongoing condition of the Jewish people (vv. 3–5). First, Paul is in "great sorrow" (also translated "great grief"),[35] λύπη ... μεγάλη. He is in a sorrowful

---

because of the interconnectedness of the statement which involves both Christ and the Holy Spirit (found to be in the dative case—Χριστῷ and πνεύματι ἁγίῳ) in verse 1. A brief amplification of this concept can be found in the writings of Lenski, *Interpretation of St. Paul's Epistle to the Romans*, 582.

30. Fitzmyer, *Romans*, 543.

31. MacArthur, *Romans 9–16*, 10; Schreiner, *Romans*, 479; and Cranfield, *Epistle to the Romans*, 452, all use the expression of witnesses, much as MacArthur did in his commentary. However, the connotation does lend to the idea of separation as MacArthur's phrase does as well.

32. Plumer, *Commentary on Romans*, 455.

33. Wallace, *Greek Grammar*, 310. Wallace does not state categorically these two nominatives as predicates; however, the possibility is allowed for, and one can affirm this, by the structure of the sentence.

34. Wallace, *Greek Grammar*, 459–60.

35. Shedd, *Commentary on Romans*, 273; Sanday and Headlam, *Epistle to the Romans*, 227; Cranfield, *Epistle to the Romans*, 453; Sneen, "Root, the Remnant, and the Branches," 398; and Dunn, *Romans 9–16*, 523.

Exegetical Understanding of Romans 9:1–5

state of mind,[36] compounded by the rejection of Jesus as Messiah by the Jewish people.[37]

Second, Paul finds himself in a position of "constant distress (ἀδιά-λειπτο ὀδύνη)." What exactly was this distress that Paul was undergoing on a constant basis? Many possibilities are up for consideration:

- Paul is expressing a physical state and not simply a mental frame-of-mind.[38]
- Paul's distress is positive, because even though he is in pain, it is a pain which can co-exist with the emotion of joy found in Romans 8.[39] This possibility is supported by the thought that "suffering together with Christ is part and parcel of the relationship with Christ that fills him with exultation (8:17). The torment caused by Israel's fall is part of the suffering he bears for the sake of Jesus."[40]
- Perhaps, Paul senses the reality and "anguish of a final separation."[41]
- A final interpretation is that ἀδιάλειπτο ὀδύνη is similar to the "apocalyptic birth-pangs" found in Mark 13:8.[42] In other words, Paul is expressing the agony that one would find in a woman giving birth, but yet not being confident that his labor will result in the joy of the salvation of his people.

Truth and potential could be found in all of the interpretations listed. However, Liddon, Schlatter, and Sneen provide the best entrance in exegeting the crucial verse of the passage—verse 3. This potential is

---

36. Sanday and Headlam, *Epistle to the Romans*, 273; Lenski, *Interpretation of St. Paul's Epistle to the Romans*, 582; and Cranfield, *Epistle to the Romans*, 453.

37. Shedd, *Commentary on Romans*, 273.

38. Cranfield, *Epistle to the Romans*, 453.

39. Liddon, *Explanatory Analysis*, 148.

40. Schlatter, *Romans*, 201.

41. Epp, "Jewish-Gentile Continuity in Paul," 81. Two things to be noted about this article in relationship to understanding the passage as it relates to Epp's commentary are: (1) Epp notes that ojduvnh is used only here and in Acts 20:38 when Paul bids farewell to the Ephesian church; and (2) Epp is influenced by his dissertation supervisor, Krister Stendahl, who is noted for a dual covenantal perspective. Johnson, "New Testament Understanding," 229 n. 5.

42. Sneen, "Root, the Remnant, and the Branches," 399.

especially evident when one considers that the depth of sorrow and pain expressed by Paul has a parallel passage in the Old Testament—Isaiah 53 and the picture of the Suffering Servant.[43]

PAUL'S OFFER OF SPIRITUAL SACRIFICE DEMONSTRATES THE EXTENT OF HIS LOVE FOR HIS OWN PEOPLE (9:3)

> [3] For I could wish myself to be accursed from Christ for my brothers my kin according to (the) flesh.

Verse 3 is a crucial moment in Paul's lament. One finds in this verse a verb which must be identified and examined, an infinitive phrase, and five nouns; however, this verse also can be seen as revolving around two small prepositions—ἀπό (from) and ὑπὲρ (for). Through these two prepositions, one is able to see what Paul is willing to relinquish, and for whom he is willing to sacrifice. However, structural analysis of the verse is required before one should seek to examine the meaning of it.

As mentioned previously, this verse in particular would have brought the parallel offer of Moses' willingness to sacrifice his life for the people to the minds of many Jewish people. However, F. F. Bruce points out that Paul was willing to "welcome perdition," while Moses was only willing to die for his people.[44] This welcoming of eternal judgment, and all the suffering it entailed, should eliminate the lingering vestiges of thought that Paul advocated a concept of dual covenantalism—the idea that Gentiles are saved through Jesus, and the Jews through the law of Moses.[45]

Paul's Willingness to be Accursed from[46] *Christ*

The phrase, "For I could wish[47] myself to be accursed (ηὐχόμην γὰρ ἀνάθεμα αὐτο ἐγώ)," leaves little room for any other exegetical outcome

---

43. Osborne, *Romans*, 236; and Dunn, *Romans 9–16*, 523–24.

44. Bruce, *Letter of Paul to the Romans*, 174.

45. Hall, *Christian Anti-Semitism*, 120–21. Hall considers the ἀνάθεμα as not a permanent condition of being "cut off" from God, but only a temporary one until the fulfillment of the Gentiles occurs. Johnson, *Reading Romans*, 242–43, rebukes any proposition of this contention, noting the obvious when he states, "Why would Paul be willing to abandon his own salvation because of a mere theological understanding on the part of his fellow-Jews?"

46. The purpose of the italics for *from* is to emphasize the significance of the preposition "ἀπό."

47. An alternate translation to "wish" is "pray." Cranfield, *Epistle to the Romans*, 454–

than the realization that, apart from Christ, the Jewish people, and consequently all people, are destined to be separated eternally from Messiah Jesus. The reality of this destiny is first found in a brief historical analysis of the verb, "ηὐχόμην."

As a professor who teaches history and English at Arlington Baptist College, I love studying the historical background and etymology of a word. History is not often appreciated or understood by those whose high school history teacher often went by the name "Coach." However, history is important, and if we do not understand the background of a concept, we will miss the true story of the passage.

The history of εὔχομαι (could wish) in the Greek, and specifically the Homeric era, dealt primarily with a general appeal to a deity.[48] The appeal was accompanied by a sacrifice to the gods in the hope that the supplicant's gift would appease them.[49] However, the importance of the word in the cultic sphere became less pronounced over time.[50]

In the Old Testament, the idea of "wish" or "pray" took on more significant meaning as it was addressing the divine.[51] The idea of "wish" was not present in the Septuagint version of the Old Testament,[52] although the concept was found in the expression of "asking from God."[53] The bridge of the intertestamental period for εὔχομαι (lexical form of ηὐχόμην) brings the concept of "wish" back to the forefront, even though "pray" still played a prominent role.[54]

In the New Testament, εὔχομαι finds its way back to a sense of the "wish" concept. However, this is only possible when the object of the address is God,[55] and even then, the verb is only used a few times in the New Testament.[56] The primary example of "pray" or "wish" finds a presence in

---

57, prefers "pray," but Dunn, *Romans 9–16*, 524, allows for "wish." The ESV, NIV, NASB, NKJV, and KJV all use the word "wish."

48. Balz, "εὔχομαι," *EDNT*: II, 89; and Kittel, ed., "εὔχομαι," *TDNT*: II, 775–76; and Brown, "προσεύχομαι," *NIDNTT*: II, 862.

49. Brown, "προσεύχομαι," *NIDNTT*: II, 862.

50. Kittel, ed., "εὔχομαι," *TDNT*: II, 777.

51. Brown, "προσεύχομαι," *NIDNTT*: 862–63.

52. Balz, "εὔχομαι," *EDNT*: II, 89.

53. Kittel, ed., "εὔχομαι," *TDNT*: II, 785.

54. Kittel, ed., "εὔχομαι," *TDNT*: II, 783.

55. Balz, "εὔχομαι," *EDNT*: II, 89; and Brown, "προσεύχομαι," *NIDNTT*: II, 867.

56. Balz, "εὔχομαι," *EDNT*: II, 89; and Brown, "προσεύχομαι," *NIDNTT*: II, 867.

the Lord's Prayer of Matthew 6,[57] as reflected in the Latin Vulgate.[58] C. E. B. Cranfield notes that Paul's use of εὔχομαι is restricted by the fact that it can never come to pass.[59]

Therefore, Wallace is correct when he considers this to be a verb indicating potentiality, as it presupposes what could be—but not what actually is—going to occur.[60] Further, he is correct in his statement that this imperfect verb is also conative. However, Wallace's translation, "For I could *almost* wish,"[61] is less than desirable, because the use of the word "almost" implies that Paul only considered the possibility.

Douglas Moo's premise indicates a position that would be in various degrees of agreement with Cranfield and Wallace when he writes that he would "ascribe a hypothetical nuance to the imperfect tense" of the word.[62] A. T. Robertson would have concurred with Wallace and Cranfield, for his translation of ηὐχόμην is seen idiomatically as "I was on the point of wishing."[63] However, James Denney believes that "the form of expression implies that the wish had actually been conceived."[64] Therefore, and based upon Wallace, an important question to ask in interpreting this passage is, would the tenor of the whole passage be lost if ηὐχόμην was translated as "I could almost wish"? This is important in light of a possible follow-up question—namely, why would Paul be in "great sorrow" or "constant distress" over a consideration?

---

57. Kittel, ed., "εὔχομαι," *TDNT*: II, 803.

58. Cranfield, *Epistle to the Romans*, 454.

59. Cranfield, *Epistle to the Romans*, 455–56.

60. Wallace, *Greek Grammar*, 451–52. See also, Lenski, *Interpretation of St. Paul's Epistle to the Romans*, 583, for an affirmation of Wallace's position. Cranfield, *Epistle to the Romans*, 455, lists four possible interpretations: (1) the verb is indicating "an action in progress in past time"; (2) a connotative imperfect that is "an action attempted but not accomplished"; (3) prayer capable of coming to pass, but expressed in vague terminology; or (4) prayer is impossible to grant, but a prayer that Paul would pray if possible. Cranfield's amplification of the verb provides an alternative understanding of Wallace's connotative definition; however, this writer sees Wallace's understanding to be the more correct understanding of connotative verbs.

61. Wallace, *Greek Grammar*, 550–52.

62. Moo, *Epistle to the Romans*, 558–59.

63. Robertson, *Word Pictures in the New Testament*, 4:380.

64. Denney, *St. Paul's Epistle to the Romans*, 657; and see also Kim, *God, Israel, and the Gentiles*, 101–2.

Exegetical Understanding of Romans 9:1–5

The more accurate translation is the one noted above by the paper's writer—"I could wish myself." This connotation provides for the inference that Paul not only considered this option in the past, but also still continued to consider it, even at the time of the writing of the epistle. However, it was only a consideration and not something that Paul admits in his own words (8:31–39) that he could have done.[65]

However, his wish was for something that few could even imagine, "ἀνάθεμα εἶναι … ἀπὸ τοῦ Χριστοῦ (to be accursed from Christ)." The word "ἀνάθεμα," came originally from two Greek words, "ἀνα"ν and "τίθημι," meaning "that which is set up" specifically for sacrifice to the gods.[66] The Septuagint translated this concept in relation to the Hebrew word (*hērem*) for "ban" and for "punishment."[67] Therefore, the concept of ἀνάθεμα, tied together with the adverbial infinitive (εἶναι) should be seen in the original languages as a desire for banishment or separation from the noun governed by the preposition "ἀπό," which is Christ himself.[68]

The correct translation for this passage is as noted above, "For I could wish myself to be accursed from Christ." This translation allows one to see that Paul was willing to be turned over to the consequences of "divine wrath" or "devoted to destruction," if it would mean the salvation of the Jews.[69] In other words, Paul's love for Christ was so grand, and his passion for the Jewish people so enormous, that even though he understood what would be the possible consequence, he was still willing to take the march to damnation for the salvation of someone else.[70] John Calvin probably summarized Paul's heart and willingness best when he wrote, "So Paul did

---

65. Gaebelein, *Romans-Galatians*, 102; Schreiner, *Romans*, 479–80; Shedd, *Commentary on Romans*, 273; Morris, *Epistle to the Romans*, 347; and Fitzmyer, *Romans*, 544.

66. Aust and Müller, "Curse, Insult, Fool (ἀνάθεμα)," 413.

67. Aust and Müller, "Curse, Insult, Fool (ἀνάθεμα)," 413–14.

68. Martin Luther discounted those who attempted to say that this expression of separation should be seen as reflective of Paul's state before the Damascus Road experience. Luther listed six reasons why this interpretation would have been impossible, including the idea that ἀνάθεμα for Paul before Christ was directed toward Jesus and his followers and not the idea of being separated "from." Pauck, *Luther*, 260–61.

69. Das, *Paul and the Jews*, 102; Kreloff, *God's Plan for Israel*, 20; Piper, *Justification of God*, 44–45; Bell, *Provoked to Jealousy*, 173; Sanday and Headlam, *Epistle to the Romans*, 228; and Cranford, "Election and Ethnicity," 31.

70. Schreiner, "Corporate and Individual Election in Romans 9," 374.

not connect God's election with his wish, but the remembrance of that being passed by, he was *wholly intent* on the salvation of the Jews."[71]

Paul's Openness to Face Perdition for His Earthly Brothers

The separation "from Christ" to which Paul was willing to subject himself was for none other than "my brothers, my kin (ὑπὲρ τῶν ἀδελφῶν μου τῶν συγγενῶν μου κατὰ σάρκα)."[72] Since the time of the Patristic commentators, the reality that this was referring to the Jewish people and not the replacement theology concept of "the church" has been acknowledged. Surprisingly enough, it is Origen in his *Commentary on the Epistle to the Romans* who wrote, "Why be surprised if, when Christ became a curse for his servants, one of his servants should become a curse for his brethren?"[73]

The reality that it was the Jewish people for whom Paul was willing to experience damnation is emphasized by the statements of "my brothers" and "my kin," with "my kin." Perhaps, Paul used this repetition to remove all doubt as to whom he was referring, because as a believer in Christ, he was a part of the family of God as well.[74] While stating that "the condition is unreal," Brendan Byrne acknowledged that Paul's heart and willingness to sacrifice for his own people "underlines the strength of feeling persisting throughout the entire section of the letter devoted to this issue (cf. 10:1; 11:1)."[75]

---

71. Calvin, *Epistle of Paul the Apostle to the Romans*, 335.

72. Witherington and Hyatt, *Paul's Letter to the Romans*, 250; and Moo, *Epistle to the Romans*, 559. A contrary view regarding whether or not that Paul is referring to the non-believing Jewish population is provided by Chae, *Paul as Apostle to the Gentiles*, 250. Chae refuses to agree with John Piper's view (23–24, 45, 64) that the people of Romans 9:3 and the recipients of the subsequent privileges of 9:4–5 are unbelieving Jews. Chae believes instead that the privileges belong to all Jewish people, Christian or not, and therefore no special bond or privilege exists of Paul's heart-longing for the unbelieving Jewish population.

73. Bray, *Romans*, 245.

74. Schreiner, *Romans*, 480–81; Cranfield, *Epistle to the Romans*, 458–59; Fitzmyer, *Romans*, 544–45; Morris, *Epistle to the Romans*, 347–48; and Dunn, *Romans 9–16*, 525.

75. Byrne, *Romans*, 285.

THE PEOPLE FOR WHOM PAUL WAS WILLING TO BE ACCURSED WERE THE JEWISH PEOPLE (9:4–5)

> ⁴ who are Israelites, whose is the adoption and the glory and the covenants and the law and the worship and the promises, ⁵ whose (are) the forefathers and from whom (is) Christ according to the flesh, who (is) over all God blessed for eternity, amen.

The first three verses of this passage elaborate on the pain of Paul's heart and the extent to which he was willing to go for the salvation of the Jewish people. Verse 4 details both the identity of the Jewish people and the blessings that have been accounted to them by God as His chosen people. The fifth verse concludes the passage by reminding the readers of just why the relationship of Jesus to the Jewish people is so important, and finally the relationship of Christ to God.

Paul's Statement Regarding the Inalienable Rights of the Israelites

The issue of whether the phrase "who are Israelites (οἵτινὲ εἰσιν Ἰσραηλῖται)" in this passage are the ethnic people group known as Jews, or "the church,"[76] will be discussed in greater detail in the third section of the book. However, the formulation of an answer must begin here, as this is the verse in which the opportunities are listed for the "Israelites."[77] Calvin emphasized the importance of developing a fully formed answer to this question, because of the emphasis Paul used in designating them as Israelites.[78] Therefore, this is not a time for trying to find an explanation in which both the nation of Israel and Christians could find a place in this verse.[79] This is a book that will categorically define verses 4–5 as referring to the nation of Israel.

---

76. Munck, *Christ and Israel*, 30. Munck considered these gifts toward Israel as a reminder of a glorious past and not something which could be claimed or assumed today.

77. Schreiner, *Romans*, 475, 483. Schreiner views the Church as the true Israel, but does not believe that all the rights for the ethnic Israel have been lost, for God must keep his promises.

78. Calvin, *Epistle of Paul the Apostle to the Romans*, 538. Calvin found the emphatic quality in Paul's choice of using a relative pronoun, as opposed to a causative adverb to begin the verse enlightening.

79. Sanday and Headlam, *Epistle to the Romans*, 229; and Aageson, "Typology, Correspondence, and the Application of Scripture in Romans 9–11," 54–55.

J. C. Beker concurs with Calvin, at least on the idea that Paul is purposely clarifying and defining to whom he is referring. Beker notes that Paul returns to the ancient term for the nation of Israel,[80] "a sacred term denoting the chosen community of God."[81] Andrew Das furthers this thought by pointing out that it would be contradictory for Paul to lament the separated condition of Israel, if this Israel was the church, or perhaps a subgroup of the nation of Israel. Das believes that a reader must look at the entirety of Israel to understand to whom Paul is referring in Rom 9:1–5, especially verses 4–5.[82]

Therefore, the gifts enumerated in verse 4 are for the nation of Israel alone. The privileges follow a specific pattern of six blessings, divided into two columns, with the first, second, fourth, and fifth privileges in the singular form, while the third and sixth blessings are plural.[83] John Piper believes that Paul chose this pattern for a specific purpose, and that it was one that was known and "traditional" in form and structure.[84]

The Spiritual Privileges of Being the Chosen People

The first privilege of being an "Israelite" is the idea of "adoption (υἱοθεσία)," an adoption that is built on the premise of "grace," and not on worthiness or strength.[85] For Israel had never been the largest, grandest, or strongest

---

80. Beker, "Romans 9–11," 49.

81. Robinson, "Salvation of Israel," 83; Longenecker, "Different Answers to Different Issues," 97; Bell, *Provoked to Jealousy*, 173; Cranfield, *Epistle to the Romans*, 460; Cranford, "Election and Ethnicity," 31; Fitzmyer, *Romans*, 545; and Gaebelein, Romans-*Galatians*, 102.

82. Das, *Paul and the Jews*, 89.

83. Das, *Paul and the Jews*, 20–21; and Osborne, *Romans*, 238. Additionally, Piper notes that all the nouns are of the feminine case, and are connected with the conjunction "καί." Consequently, it should also be noted that, by necessity, the syntax for all six is the same–predicate nominative.

84. Piper, *Justification of God*, 21. Bell, *Provoked to Jealousy*, 174–75, concurs with Piper's assumption that this was a form and structure which Paul had used many times before.

85. Cranfield, *Epistle to the Romans*, 461; Williamson, *Guest in the House of Israel*, 102; Jowett, *Epistles of St. Paul* 275; Garrett, *Systematic Theology*, 2:288–89; Dunn, *Romans 9–16*, 526; and MacArthur, *Romans 9-16*, 13. MacArthur, unfortunately, instead of focusing on the graciousness of God in his choosing of this small, nomadic band of people, chooses to focus instead on their failures as God's chosen people. Perhaps, this is why it made it easier for him to consider the Jewish people as "temporarily set aside."

nation in the world (Deut 7:7–11); however, God still chose them to be the people of God and the forerunners of the Messiah (see v. 5).

The second privilege of being a chosen people is the reality of "glory (δόξα)." This privilege is a difficult concept for contemporary Jewish people to recognize in the light and reality of two thousand years of history since the advent of Christ. The term "glory" would be a problem if one viewed this word from a human vantage point; however, it is not a problem when one realizes that the focus of glory should not be on the recipient, but upon the giver of it.[86] This is given credence by the Hebrew (Old Testament) concept of glory, *kabod*, which indicates the heaviness of the Lord.[87] Dunn and Piper agree with the Old Testament analysis of God's glory, but also remind the reader that δόξα for Israel is still to come, because of the eschatological promises of God manifested to the nations "through Israel."[88] Piper explains this eschatological hope by reminding the reader that δόξα, along with υἱοθεσία, offers a "look to the future with roots in the past."[89]

The third privilege of being a member of the Jewish people is "covenants (αἱ διαθῆκαι)." According to Calvin, a covenant "is that which is expressed in distinct and accustomed words, and contains a mutual stipulation, as that which was made with Abraham."[90] Additionally, Calvin makes a clear distinction between the covenants mentioned and the promises indicated in verse 4;[91] however, to affirm Calvin's position is difficult. In contrast, Thomas Schreiner tries to incorporate the two words "διαθῆκαι" and "ἐπαγγελίαι."[92] In this scenario, one should agree with Calvin, as opposed to Schreiner. "Covenants" are connected in the feminine plural sense. They are disconnected, because one is talking about

---

86. Bell, *Provoked to Jealousy*, 176–77; Cranfield, *Epistle to the Romans*, 461–62; and Hodge, *Epistle to the Romans*, 299.

87. *Hebrew and English Lexicon of the Old Testament*, s.v. "kabod."

88. Dunn, *Romans 9–16*, 526–27; and Piper, *Justification of God*, 33–34.

89. Piper, *Justification of God*, 34.

90. Calvin, *Epistle of Paul the Apostle to the Romans*, 340.

91. Calvin, *Epistle of Paul the Apostle to the Romans*, 340.

92. Schreiner, *Romans*, 484–85. Bell, *Provoked to Jealousy*, 177, somewhat supports Schreiner's position, but stops short of a complete affirmation. However, Bell prefers to focus on the future aspect of the covenants, and not the ones from Old Testament past.

commitment, and the other (promises) is speaking of "what we meet with everywhere in Scripture."[93]

One primary issue to be determined in this section is why Paul used the plural form for covenant as opposed to the singular. The more common understanding of why Paul chose the plural form of the word is that he was focusing on the totality of the covenant itself, while noting the various renewals or "addendums" he made with Moses and David.[94] An excellent explanation in support of the plural form is the fact that the plural avoids the confusion of designation to which covenant Paul was referring the Noahic, Abrahamic, Mosaic, or Davidic covenant.[95]

The fourth privilege of being an Israelite is "law (νομοθεσία)." The history of the law and the Jewish people is well-established from the time of Mount Sinai (Exodus 19). Therefore, this "law" should be considered an obvious privilege of the Jewish people. Israel was able to have God be their personal "instructor,"[96] and even though the Jewish people at the time of Paul had placed the law above the prophecies of the Messiah found within the law,[97] this giving of the law was a blessing bestowed to the Jewish people.[98]

The fifth privilege of the Jewish people is "worship"[99] or "service (λατρεία)"[100] to God. The root concept of the Greek understanding of the word is a sense of wages or reward for service in an environment

---

93. Calvin, *Epistle of Paul the Apostle to the Romans*, 340.

94. Hendriksen, *New Testament Commentary*, 312; Guerra, "Romans," 228; Lenski, *Interpretation of St. Paul's Epistle to the Romans*, 585; Bruce, *Letter of Paul to the Romans*, 175; Morris, *Epistle to the Romans*, 348; Sanday and Headlam, *Epistle to the Romans*, 230–31; and Dunn, *Romans 9–16*, 527.

95. Gaebelein, *Romans-Galatians*, 102; and Moo, *Epistle to the Romans*, 563. Douglas Moo specifically believes that the concept of covenants refers to the covenants God instituted in the Old Testament via Noah, Abraham, Moses, and David. Further, Moo notes that the plural form of covenant (αἱ διαθῆκαι) was not an unusual choice for Paul, for he had used the plural in Ephesians 2:12 to "mark Israel as God's special people...."

96. Fitzmyer, *Romans*, 546.

97. Sanday and Headlam, *Epistle to the Romans*, 231.

98. Cranfield, *Epistle to the Romans*, 463; and Bell, *Provoked to Jealousy*, 177.

99. Balz, "λατρεία," *EDNT*: II, 344; Wright, *Climax of the Covenant*, 237; and Moo, *Epistle to the Romans*, 564.

100. Hess, "λατρεία"; Brown, "προσεύχομαι," *NIDNTT*: III, 549; and Strathmann, "λατρεία," *TDNT*: IV, 59.

of worship.¹⁰¹ The Hebrew concept of the "worship," as found in the Old Testament Septuagint, is based on the priestly functions or formal acts of worship to Yahweh (יהוה) by the Levites.¹⁰²

Many English versions have translated λατρεία as "temple service" or simply "service";¹⁰³ however, the preference should be what is engendered by the idea of worship.¹⁰⁴ Bell, as well as Sanday and Headlam, maintain the concept of "service," specifically, that "service" related to the sacrificial system of the Old Testament for translating λατρεία.¹⁰⁵ Perhaps, it should be allowed that both terms are acceptable. Garrett notes that no distinction exists between "reverential service" (deeds) and "worship" (spontaneous expressions of joy) to God.¹⁰⁶

The sixth privilege listed by Paul relating to ethnic Israel is "the promises (αἱ ἐπαγγελίαι)." Paul does not specify the type or extent of "the promises," but two primary views exist to this issue. Some believe that "αἱ ἐπαγγελίαι," mentioned in Romans 9:4 are primarily, even strictly, Messianic in nature.¹⁰⁷ James D. G. Dunn prefers to view the promises as primarily dealing with the Patriarchs (Abraham, Isaac, and Jacob);¹⁰⁸ however, he allows the concept that the promises were fulfilled in Jesus.¹⁰⁹ The latter view is probably the more correct interpretation of "the promises," specifically in the sense of the plural form of the word. Therefore, Piper probably expressed the all-encompassing sense of the fulfillment of the promises of God when he wrote, "So we can see that for Paul the

---

101. Brown, "προσεύχομαι," *NIDNTT*: III, 549; and Strathmann, "λατρεία," *TDNT*: IV, 58–59.

102. Brown, "προσεύχομαι," *NIDNTT*: III, 549–50; Strathmann, "λατρεία," *TDNT*: IV, 58–62; Balz, "λατρεία," *EDNT*: II, 344; and Denney, *St. Paul's Epistle to the Romans*, 657.

103. NASB, HCSB translate it to read "temple service." The KJV and NKJV translate it as "service," and the NIV has it read as "temple worship." The ASV translates it to read "service (of God)."

104. Garrett, *Systematic Theology*, 2:592. James Leo Garrett gives the noun in question two primary interpretations—"worship" or "reverential service." The following English versions agree with the term "worship:" ESV, TEV, RSV, and NRSV.

105. Bell, *Provoked to Jealousy*, 178; and Sanday and Headlam, *Epistle to the Romans*, 231.

106. Garrett, *Systematic Theology*, 2:592.

107. Sanday and Headlam, *Epistle to the Romans*, 231; and Schreiner, *Romans*, 487.

108. Dunn, *Romans 9–16*, 528.

109. Hendriksen, *New Testament Commentary*, 313–14; Cranfield, *Epistle to the Romans*, 464; and Bell, *Provoked to Jealousy*, 178.

promises of God flow together into a summation of all the good that God can possibly offer his people."[110]

The Spiritual Legacy of Being the Chosen People Included the Promise of the Messiah

On the surface, the final verse in this passage appears to be a straightforward declaration of Jesus' humanity and his physical lineage/connection to the Jewish people. However, and as will be illustrated, the verse also contains a potential Pauline declaration that Jesus is not only the Messiah, He is also God.

The first matter of this verse for discussion is perhaps the least complicated. Jesus was born as a Jewish male[111] who ministered to the Jewish people.[112] The argument for this fact is based on the words of Paul himself, "whose (are) the forefathers (ὧν οἱ πατέρε)," referring to his descending from the Patriarchs, as well as "according to the flesh (τὸ κατὰ σάρκα)," which refers to the physical lineage of Jesus (see Matt 1:1–25).[113] This unique reality of Jesus, as Jew and subsequently God (see next paragraph), "is the most sublime gift that could have been bestowed upon Israel, and it fulfills all the gracious gifts previously given."[114]

The second issue in this verse is far more complicated and depends primarily upon whether a translator places a comma or inserts a period after "τὸ κατὰ σάρκα (according to the flesh)." This punctuation choice will determine whether one believes that Paul is making a statement regarding Jesus as God, or has simply stopped his declaration of love for the Jewish people and their legacy as Israelites to begin a short praise (doxology) to God. The argument cannot be solved by going to the origi-

---

110. Piper, *Justification of God*, 39.

111. Cranfield, *Epistle to the Romans*, 464; Schlatter, *Romans*, 202; and Piper, *Justification of God*, 43.

112. MacArthur, *Romans 9–16*, 15; and Longenecker, "Different Answers to Different Issues," 105.

113. MacArthur, *Romans 9–16*, 15. The use of relative pronoun (ὧν) causes one to realize that verse 5 is referring back to the "Israelites" of verse 4. Black, *Learn to Read New Testament Greek*, 155–57.

114. Schlatter, *Romans*, 202. This writer disagrees with the idea that one could assume by the possible replacement theology statement "fulfills all the graciously gifts previously given." This writer is not stating that Schlatter is a replacement theologian; however, the sense of fulfilled gifts which Schlatter mentions could lead others to believe that the previous gifts of God have now been made null and void.

Exegetical Understanding of Romans 9:1–5

nal manuscripts, because for the most part they were "destitute of any sort of punctuation."[115] To determine what the historical perspective on the issue has to say, one would have to go to the early Church Fathers. Sanday and Headlam list Tertullian, Cyprian, Athanasius, Gregory of Nyssa, John Chrysostom, and Origen as advocates regarding a proclamation of Jesus' deity.[116] Augustine, through cross-referencing Psalm 110:1, advocated a declaration of Jesus' divinity.[117] However, Cyril of Alexandria and Diodorus believed it was a doxology of praise to God,[118] and they were joined by Ambrosiaster in this view.[119]

Again, no distinction is available through the historical records. Further, modern translations of Scripture are equally divided on the issue. A comma is used in the NASB, KJV, HCSB, NKJV, and NIV, while a period or no punctuation at all is used in the New Jerusalem Bible (NJB), Revised Standard Version (RSV), and Today's English Version (TEV).[120] Bruce Metzger provides a rationale for choosing a comma placement instead of a period:

- "(1) the structure of the entire verse advocates a proclamation and not a doxology;
- (2) the reality that ὤν would be 'superfluous' if the expression was a doxology;
- (3) the presumption that 'Pauline doxologies' always 'attach themselves' to something which precedes the doxology;
- (4) the verbal construction does not lend itself to a doxology; and
- (5) Paul's lament over the eternal condition of the Jewish people would not easily lend itself to becoming a doxology of praise to God."[121]

---

115. Metzger, "Punctuation of Rom 9:5," 97; and Sanday and Headlam, *Epistle to the Romans*, 233.

116. Sanday and Headlam, *Epistle to the Romans*, 234. See also, Bray, specifically related to Origen, *Romans*, 246–47.

117. Bray, *Romans*, 247.

118. Liddon, *Explanatory Analysis*, 151.

119. Bray, *Romans*, 247.

120. *Greek New Testament*, 543. For another analysis of which versions use or do not use a comma in translation, see also, Barnhouse, *God's Covenants*, 19–20.

121. Metzger, *Textual Commentary*, 521–22.

Since the historical, manuscript, and translation evidence does not provide a clear-cut answer to the issue of whether Paul was making a statement concerning the deity of Christ in verse 5,[122] one is required to examine the two points that Paul is trying to make in the passage as a whole. The first point is to identify the man Jesus, and the second is why a relationship with Jesus as Messiah would cause Paul to be willing to sacrifice all for the Jewish people who had not yet believed in Jesus.

The answer to both questions will be examined in greater depth in further chapters; however, it is important to note here that Paul's act of sacrificial love is comparable to what Moses was willing to do in the wilderness (Exod 32:31–32). This willingness for self-sacrifice, along with Paul's own acceptance of the sacrifice of Jesus on the cross, consequently must be related to his recognition that Jesus is God[123] (Acts 13:33–35; Phil 2:5–11; 1 Tim 4:1), and that he came to save Jewish people, the chosen people of God.

The lament of Rom 9:1–5 shows a Paul who experiences such a burden for his own brothers and sisters that he was willing to experience the fires of hell if they had become believers in Messiah Jesus. Because of the certainty and security of salvation found in Rom 8:31–39, he knows he cannot; however, he would have volunteered had it been possible. This willingness is an action of love that is inconceivable to many today. In fact, my Baptist father once said that most people behave under the operation of the old adage, "us four and no more."

---

122. One aspect of the argument is the Pauline use of doxologies. A full analysis of this issue will not be addressed; however, the majority argument is that Paul's doxologies still refer to the antecedent to the one who was addressed previously (i.e., the Christ). Therefore, if this is a doxology, the addressee is Jesus of Nazareth. See, Cranfield, *Epistle to the Romans*, 467; Schreiner, *Romans*, 488; and Sanday and Headlam, *Epistle to the Romans*, 234. However, a large number of modern commentators prefer to view it as a self-contained praise of and recognition that Jesus is indeed God. See, Metzger, "Punctuation of Rom 9:5," 112; Sanday and Headlam, *Epistle to the Romans*, 238; Das, *Paul and the Jews*, 84; Calvin, *Epistle of Paul the Apostle to the Romans*, 342–43; Brown, *Jesus*, 22; Schreiner, *Romans*, 487–89; Schlatter, *Romans*, 202–3; Hendriksen, *New Testament Commentary*, 315; and Gaebelein, *Romans-Galatians*, 103.

123. Moo, *Epistle to the Romans*, 566–68; Witherington and Hyatt, *Paul's Letter to the Romans*, 251–52; and Schlatter, *Romans*, 201–3. Johnson, *Reading Romans*, 157–58, posits an alternate position, for while Johnson affirms that, in other passages, Paul referenced Jesus as God, he prefers the period as opposed to the comma placement, for he sees this section of verse 5 as a doxology and not a declaration.

I did not understand the depth of Paul's burden until I met my friend Josef. He survived the Holocaust, including the loss of his whole family, and arrived in America with the head knowledge of a rabbi, but the heart of an agnostic. My friendship with Josef happened shortly after I moved to New York City. Pages could be written about our friendship, including, after learning of my father's death, his quiet assent that a heaven existed. However, bottom line, he was my friend, and I loved him dearly.

He died in 2002—an old man with no family, few friends, and, as far as I know—without Messiah Jesus. I had witnessed to him every at every opportunity, including the last time I saw him, shortly before his death. To this day, I still grieve for Josef—grieve as a friend would for someone who dies, and a mourning for one you are fairly confident that you will never see again in eternity. I do not know if I could even today say the words of Rom 9:3, but I would give anything and everything to see Josef one more time. As real as my burden is, Paul's was even greater.

PART THREE

Introduction to Chapters 5 through 7

I AM THE DAUGHTER of a Baptist preacher and his wife. My paternal grandfather was a Baptist deacon. My maternal grandmother taught a ladies' Sunday School class until she became a homebound invalid. I am predominantly Irish on both sides of my family tree. What does this biographical trip down memory lane have to do with this book? It just goes to illustrate that I come from a long line of opinionated individuals. By this point in the book, I do not believe you would be surprised to discover that I was a state quarter-finalist in high school debate and state runner-up in extemporaneous speaking.

Therefore, these chapters are right down my genetic predisposition to love controversy. Was Paul an anti-Semite? Did someone else really write this controversial Thessalonians passage and place it in the epistle to give Jewish hatred a legitimized voice? Does Paul teach in Romans that two ways to heaven exist—one for the Jewish people and Jesus for everyone else? Does Paul actually advocate that the Jewish people lost their status as "Chosen Ones," and it now belongs to the Church? Or, did he perhaps even advocate that the Old Testament (i.e., Hebrew Scriptures) was really always and only about the church, and Israel was merely a stand-in until the real people loved by God showed up? All these are questions to stir the fancy of an argumentative soul like myself; however, all are questions that must be answered in order for God's Word and His still present call for Jewish evangelism to be heard. Thus, the only questions remaining are—are you ready to listen? What will you decide after you have heard?

5

Questions Regarding Interpolation and Anti-Semitism (1 Thessalonians 2:13–16)

On the "Sesame Street" that I watched as a child of the 1970s, a moment/vignette was always included, in which the child was supposed to pick out which one of the four pictures was different than the others. Sometimes it was easy—one fish as opposed to three birds. Sometimes it was difficult like when you had a kangaroo, a koala bear, a fox, and a possum (HINT: kangaroo is the only one with a pouch). Likewise, 1 Thessalonians 2:13–16 can appear to be an anomaly to the rest of the letter—a series of expressions designed to assist in spiritual growth (2:1–12; 3:1–8; 4:1–12).[1] This section of 2:13–16 does not express an attitude of thanksgiving, but rather a diatribe against the persecutors of the faithful, by the oppressors known as "the Jews."[2]

F. F. Bruce offers a solution of 2:13, beginning a "further thanksgiving" portion,[3] but this does not solve the overall problem of Paul's use of the expression, "the Jews," or his invective description of them as killers of Christ.[4] Therefore, the questions for this section are the following: (1) Is

---

1. Green, *Letters to the Thessalonians*, 56; Best, *First and Second Epistles to the Thessalonians*, 15; and Donfried, *Paul, Thessalonica, and Early Christianity*, 77. Of note, however, is one doctrinal discourse on eschatology exists in the Thessalonian letter—4:13—5:6.

2. Holtz, "Judgment on the Jews and the Salvation of All Israel," 287. Holtz provides a long explanation related to the negative connotation of "the Jews." He ultimately summarizes it with this description: "'the Jews' means the members of the synagogue persecuting Paul as a messenger of Christ."

3. Bruce, *1 & 2 Thessalonians*, 43.

4. Sandmel, *Anti-Semitism in the New Testament?*, 14–15; van Buren, "Problem of a Christian Theology of the People Israel," 50; Manus, "Luke's Account of Paul," 35. C. U. Manus purports that Paul was alluding to an "anti-Semitic tradition" known by both the Qumran source and Mark.

the controversial passage an interpolation (a post-Pauline addition to the text)?, (2) Is Paul an anti-Semite?, or (3) Has Paul been misinterpreted for almost two thousand years?

Perhaps these questions might appear to be pedantic; however, these are very real questions in today's Christian world. As I was putting the finishing touches on the book, I took a weekend away from the laptop to stand alongside my Jewish friends and, specifically, Holocaust survivors against the vitriol of the Phelps family and Westboro Baptist Church of Topeka, Kansas.[5] Westboro "Baptist Church," while known for their protests against homosexuality and picketing the memorial services of Iraqi War soldiers with such signs as "Pray for More Dead Soldiers,"[6] also denigrates and hates the Jewish people. Included in this hate is the statement—"The Jews Killed Jesus"—and using 1 Thess 2:15 as an argument for this position.

To dismiss the ravings of the Phelps family would be easy, and we should; however, their position is either subconsciously or subtly held by many within Christian churches. Many often want to find someone, anyone, other than themselves to blame for the death of Jesus. Verse 15 in the Thessalonians passage seems to provide the perfect "fall guy"; however, more to this issue is present than meets the eye, and the issue is worth pursuing. The issue must be explored and reconciled.

ISSUE OF INTERPOLATION

Many conservative Evangelicals will automatically dismiss the concept of interpolation. However, it should be analyzed and considered as it provides the groundwork for not only determining our position on infallibility/inerrancy, but also on just what we think of Paul. Therefore, it is always a good idea, and one that I push my college students to grasp, to define our terms.

An interpolation of Scripture can be defined as inserting into the text an outside (often anonymous) theological position with the hope that the Scripture itself can provide credence or authority to the viewpoint.[7]

---

5. A full analysis of the antics and beliefs of Westboro Baptist Church, Topeka, Kansas, can be found at "Extremism in America-Westboro Baptist Church: About WBC"; Internet.

6. Batheja, "Counterprotests Drown out Westboro Baptist Members at 2 Arlington Churches"; Internet.

7. Nash, "Interpolations in the New Testament"; Internet. See also a classical definition of the word at "Interpolate"; Internet.

Questions Regarding Interpolation and Anti-Semitism

Arguments of an interpolation position for 1 Thess 2:13–16 are present in the writings of many scholars, including the Tübingen School's F. C. Baur. Due to the fact that the comparison of persecution between Judea and Thessalonica is "far-fetched," and that the wording used does not match other Pauline texts, Baur stated that the passage had "a thoroughly un-Pauline stamp."[8]

The leading modern proponents of interpolation are Daryl Schmidt and Birger Pearson. Pearson focuses on the basic incompatibilities between the other writings of Paul and 2:13–16 as his evidence for interpolation. He considers the issues that the persecution of the Judean church is mentioned only in this Pauline passage, and the wrath of v. 16c as occurring after AD 70, as proofs that would, therefore, prevent Pauline authorship.[9] Schmidt draws his argument from two areas: the length of the thanksgiving narratives, if 2:13–16 is not interpolated, and the ease in which 2:13–16 can be excised without doing any damage to the letter.[10]

Opponents of interpolation include Mikael Tellbe,[11] Karl Donfried,[12] Jon Weatherly,[13] and Jonas Holmstrand.[14] Holmstrand attacks Pearson's arguments by showing that Pearson errs in his understanding of the entire context of the passage, as well as failing to realize that, even in passages that are overtly sympathetic to the Jewish people (Rom 9:27; 10:21), one can find reprimands as it relates to their rejection of Jesus.[15] Tellbe finds no extant evidence for interpolation.[16] Donfried and Weatherly see this passage as an amplification of the suffering theme found elsewhere in

---

8. Baur, *Paul*, 87–88; Taylor, "Who Persecuted the Thessalonian Christians?," 785; and Murrell, "Human Paul," 170–72. In addition to F. C. Baur, Murrell also notes two additional interpolation advocates, Hendrikus Boers and Helmut Koester.

9. Pearson, "1 Thessalonians 2:13–16," 83, 85–86, 91.

10. Schmidt, "1 Thess 2:13–16," 269–79. Schmidt's argument is not necessarily original, but is given prior credence because of the writings of Boers, "Form Critical Study of Paul's Letters," 149–52. See also, Pearson, "1 Thessalonians 2:13–16," 91.

11. Tellbe, *Paul Between Synagogue and State*, 105.

12. Donfried, "Paul and Judaism," 244–45.

13. Weatherly, "Authenticity of 1 Thessalonians 2.13–16," 79–98, esp. 89–90.

14. Holmstrand, *Markers and Meaning in Paul*, 42–47.

15. Holmstrand, *Markers and Meaning in Paul*, 42–43.

16. Tellbe, *Paul Between Synagogue and State*, 105.

the letter, and argue that anyone who fails to receive the Messiah will be sentenced to "condemnation."[17]

Biblical scholars, therefore, often find themselves in a theological quandary, pertaining to verses 13–16. However, the answer of interpolation detracts from Paul's desire to both commend the working and living faith of the Thessalonian, as well as to illustrate the depth of depravity, which can occur when a person or people group rejects the reality that Jesus is the Messiah. Consequently, interpolation is not the approach one should take in interpreting this passage for either theological or exegetical reasons.

For example, this section begins with a καὶ . . . καὶ ἡμεῖς, and is evidence of a reciprocal show of thanksgiving.[18] In other words, this passage should be considered as a part of the overall letter. In addition, the use of the word "εὐχαριστοῦμεν" also indicates a recurrent theme found in the entire letter (1:2; 3:9; 5:18).[19] These two pieces of evidence further strengthen the argument that, while the passage is unusual in the light of the entire letter, it correlates to the epistle and, therefore, should not be considered an interpolation.[20]

A further examination of v. 16b requires one to examine the aorist verb form, ἔφθασεν φρομ φθάνω, meaning (has come)."[21] The preferred explanation is to see this aorist form as a proleptic aorist, which provides one with the sense that the wrath is present, but still coming in the eschatological sense of the word.[22] However, and regardless of the meaning of ἔφθασεν, the final section of the passage is for many biblical and theological scholars the most troubling, especially for those commentators who reject the concept of interpolation.

---

17. Weatherly, "Authenticity of 1 Thessalonians 2.13–16," 89–90; and Donfried, "Paul and Judaism," 246.

18. Frame, *Epistles of St. Paul to the Thessalonians*, 106.

19. Holmes, *1 and 2 Thessalonians*, 80; and Hiebert, *Thessalonian Epistles*, 108.

20. Hurd, "Paul Ahead of His Time," 27–33; and Murrell, "Human Paul," 74.

21. An alternate translational view is "has already come," and is supported by both advocates and opponents of interpolation. See Okeke, "I Thessalonians 2:13–16," 130; and Green, *Letters to the Thessalonians*, 149.

22. Williams, *1 and 2 Thessalonians*, 49; Frame, *Epistles of St. Paul to the Thessalonians*, 114; and Wanamaker, *Epistles to the Thessalonians*, 117.

Questions Regarding Interpolation and Anti-Semitism 65

> St. Paul's intemperate outburst against "the Jews" in 1 Thessalonians 2:14–16 has long troubled the politically reconstructed, post-Holocaust guild of *Neutestamentler*. How can the same man possibly have believed that God's wrath and definitive condemnation have "finally come upon" the Jews—only to claim elsewhere that "all Israel will be saved"?[23]

However, the root of Bockmuehl's question does not lie in whether Paul meant what he said in 1 Thess 2:16,[24] but in whether we can accept and defend that the statement is not in contradiction to other Pauline passages, and as it applies specifically to Rom 9:1–5. If one chooses to view the verses as simply, and only, representative of Paul's commitment to evangelism,[25] one limits a complete understanding of the passage. To propose a "limited condemnation" that is resolved with the destruction of the Temple in AD 70 is not appropriate,[26] as the proper choice is to examine how seemingly contradictory passages are, in fact, complementary.

The seeming contradiction is based more upon the tone than on the meaning of the passage, especially in light of all of Paul's letters. Therefore, the contradiction can be resolved, and interpolation ultimately dismissed as incorrect, by affirming the view of Charles Wanamaker who wrote, "... the majority of the Jewish people had not accepted their own messiah and ... they were positively hindering the spread of the gospel of God to non-Jews. This would account for the strong sense of frustration and antagonism found in 2:15f., without closing the door to the sort of further reflection found in Rom 9–11."[27]

THESSALONIAN ACCUSATIONS

"Wrath of God"

The wrath mentioned in 2:16b, which was discussed in chapter three, should not be regarded as simple anger, but as a wrath resulting in judgment. The question which was asked and answered in chapter three is whether the wrath is current or eschatological in nature. The view of this writer is that the evidence supports the view of a future, or eschatological

---

23. Bockmuehl, "I Thessalonians 2:14–16 and the Church in Jerusalem," 1.
24. Bockmuehl, "I Thessalonians 2:14–16 and the Church in Jerusalem," 1.
25. Schreiner, *Paul*, 473.
26. Rydelnik, "Was Paul Anti-Semitic?" 65–67.
27. Wanamaker, *Epistles to the Thessalonians*, 118.

wrath,[28] which raises a second question—who is destined for this wrath? If one believes that Paul is expressing an anti-Semitic viewpoint,[29] then all Jews—and not only "the Jews" mentioned in the passage—are destined for perdition. If one believes that Paul was referring to only those Jews who reject the gift of salvation, then the potential of hope for the Jewish people remains.[30]

Obviously, the realization of wrath is destined for those who ultimately and eternally reject the gift of Messiah Jesus—Jew or Gentile. Paul did not "mellow" down his words or "target" his words as has been suggested by Amy-Jill Levine.[31] Neither did he operate under the presumption that the church at Thessalonica would never know what he wrote to the church at Rome—and vice-versa. Paul was writing his heart, and the lament of his heart revealed itself in different ways and at different times.

Pauline Anti-Semitism

The argument stating that Paul was expressing an anti-Semitic invective begins with the concluding phrases of 2:13–16. This position would support the joint concept of being unpleasing to God and demonstrating hostility to humanity (καὶ θεῷ μὴ ἀρεσκόντων καὶ πᾶσιν ἀνθρώποις ἐναντίων).[32] F. F. Bruce considers this section to be a piece of "indiscrimi-

---

28. Donfried, *Paul, Thessalonica, and Early Christianity*, 90, 95, 204–5. Donfried finds multiple references to a future, or eschatological, sense of wrath in 1 Thessalonians (1:10; 5:2; 5:9). His eschatological sense of wrath has, however, both a present as well as a future connotation. He writes, "because of the gospel, namely, the death and resurrection of Jesus, all persons, Jews and Gentiles, stand explicitly under the wrath of God until such time that they accept His offer of new life in Christ as grace."

29. Best, *First and Second Epistles to the Thessalonians*, 122. A contrary view to Best is expressed by Hurd, "Paul Ahead of His Time," 27, 34, who believes the conflicted nature of Paul as a Jew and as a Christian left him in a dilemma as to how he should respond to his ethnic heritage, when it so obviously clashed with his spiritual one. Hurd believes that this internal conflict resulted in anger toward his "brothers and sisters," who not only rejected the Messiahship of Jesus, but also attempted to circumvent his evangelistic outreaches to the Gentiles. See also, Murrell, "Human Paul," 176, 180; and Lamp, "Is Paul Anti-Jewish?" 410–14.

30. Schreiner, *Paul*, 474; Still, *Conflict at Thessalonica*, 41, 130; Holtz, "Judgment on the Jews and the Salvation of All Israel," 286; and Marshall, *1 and 2 Thessalonians*, 83.

31. Levine, *Misunderstood Jew*, 98.

32. Bockmuehl, "1 Thessalonians 2:14–16 and the Church in Jerusalem," 14–15.

nate anti-Jewish polemic," as it was reflective of the view of the Graeco-Roman world toward the Jewish people.³³

Gene Green would disagree with Bruce, and views this expression as a continuation of Old Testament themes (Numbers 23:27; 1 Kings 3:10; Psalm 69:31).³⁴ Ernest Best agrees with Green, for he links this hostility to the Jewish fear of losing their place as the "privileged people of God."³⁵ T. Holtz expands the view of Green and Best, considering the "attack" to be a part of a common argumentative response that was common—not only in the Jewish world, but also in the ancient world as a whole.³⁶

The best conclusion is to agree with Green, Best, and Holtz as they best understand the Jewish approach to argumentation. First Thessalonians 2:13–16 was polemical in the sense of an intracultural argument between Paul the Jew and the Jewish leaders who were opposing the Gospel message, both in Judea and in Thessalonica. Paul was not expressing an anti-Semitic sentiment in 2:13–16, but instead was engaging in the Judaic style of religious engagement, which would have been both expected and respected by his Jewish opponents.³⁷ Perhaps Garry Willis describes this best as a "family quarrel."³⁸

EVALUATION OF THE INTERPOLATION AND ANTI-SEMITIC QUESTION

Ultimately, the root of the struggle in developing a proper exegetical and theological interpretation of 1 Thess 2:13–16 lies with the level of

---

33. Bruce, *1 & 2 Thessalonians*, 47.

34. Green, *Letters to the Thessalonians*, 145–46. Additionally, Green dispels Bruce's argument of an anti-Jewish polemic by stressing that Paul "limits the critique to Jewish opposition to God's mission."

35. Best, *First and Second Epistles to the Thessalonians*, 117–18.

36. Holtz, "Judgment on the Jews and the Salvation of All Israel," 285; Murrell, "Human Paul," 177; Wanamaker, *Epistles to the Thessalonians*, 118–19; and Still, *Conflict at Thessalonica*, 205.

37. Diprose, *Israel and the Church*, 33; Malherbe, *Letter to the Thessalonians*, 177–79; Rydelnik, "Was Paul an Anti-Semitic?," 63–65; and Lamp, "Is Paul Anti-Jewish?" 412.

38. Willis, *What Paul Meant*, 127. One should disagree with Willis's contention that the "Jews" in 1 Thess 2:13–16 are none other than fellow Jewish believers who are struggling with law observance; however, Willis does recognize that Paul identified himself as a "Jew's Jew" (128). This concept of Paul as a Jewish man also confuses those within Judaism who dislike Paul for their presuppositions of what he said and meant. See Shulevitz, "Was Paul a Jew?"; Internet.

personal discomfort one allows him or herself, as it relates to the eternal destination of the Jewish people. The comfortable solution would be to agree with Pearson and Schmidt and say that this section of God's Word is a mere interpolation and can, therefore, be dismissed as non-Pauline.[39] However, this solution would be nothing more than taking the "path of least resistance" and a denigration to the integrity of 1 Thessalonians that is set before us. The theological, as well as exegetical, analysis of 1 Thess 2:13–16 is that the passage is not interpolated and, thus, must be understood and interpreted in the light of its context.[40]

An alternative, but equally less than ideal solution to the problem of a potential polemic, is to surmise that Paul was speaking strictly in the human, fleshly nature and not from the Spirit of God.[41] If this was a probable solution, then two questions would need to be asked about Paul and the Word of God—(1) Was Paul's nature one of Jewish self-hatred?, and/or (2) Can the sovereign beauty of Scripture really be so human?

The final conclusion drawn by this thesis is that Paul was not an anti-Semite, and his expression of frustration in 2:13–16 is not substantially different from his expression of longing found in Rom 9:1–5.[42] As a Jewish man, Paul longed to see the salvation of his own ethnic people. This longing can be seen in the pathos of Rom 9:1–5, as well as the frustration of 1 Thess 2:13–16. In light of Paul's missionary endeavors, both emotional responses are legitimate, and both should be respected in light of their situations and circumstances. In other words, and to reflect back to the "Sesame Street" illustration at the beginning of this chapter, 1 Thess 2:13–16 is not different than the other ones, but just the same . . . with a twist.

---

39. Murrell, "Human Paul," 172–73. Murrell provides a highlight of the history of anti-Semitism and the Christian church in the last 1,900+ years as evidence that while wrong, interpolation provides a panacea to the reality of bigotry by Christendom toward the Jewish people.

40. Donfried, *Paul, Thessalonica, and Early Christianity*, 95.

41. Gager, *Origins of Anti-Semitism*, 256; and Hagner, "Paul's Quarrel with Judaism," 135–36. This solution would be significant to Gager who, as a non-Christian Jew, desires to find a solution to the waves of anti-Semitism experienced by his people throughout the ages. However, his argumentation is more idealized than exegetically or theologically sound.

42. Holtz, "Judgment on the Jews and the Salvation of All Israel," 284; Manus, "Luke's Account of Paul," 35; Horner, *Future Israel*, 142, 254; and Wanamaker, *Epistles to the Thessalonians*, 31–32.

6

Rationale and Error of Dual Covenantalism (Romans 9:1–5)

In high school, Janice was a member of Future Homemakers of America, played the flute in the band, and was manager of the volleyball team. I was involved in speech and debate, choir, and was the captain of my Academic Bowl team. Janice is a banker, Sunday School teacher, and church organist. I am a professor, writer, and missionary. We are different in a myriad of ways. We also are sisters.

Janice and I share the same parents and were raised with the same set of rules and expectations. While my parents may have had to respond to different misbehaviors with regard to my sister and me, they did not have one set of rules for Janice and another set for me. The consequences, regardless of who might have misbehaved, were the same . . . "the talk!" Believe me, "the talk" was not a fun time for anyone.

God's relationship with His children, Jewish or Gentile, is the same as it was for Jack and Barbara Downey. He is a God the Father of justice. He is a God the Father of mercy and grace. He is a God the Father who provided the same path to salvation for all humanity—Messiah Jesus. However, many use Rom 9:1–5 in an attempt to find a two-pronged plan of salvation (dual covenantalism): one for the Jewish people through the law of Moses and one for the rest of the world through Jesus Christ. Therefore, the question for this chapter is simply, does this passage provide this "salvation out?"

The question of dual covenantalism appears to present a theological schism within Christianity. While struggling with the question of just who are the present chosen people of God, traditional evangelical Christians generally operate under the assumption that only one way to the Father

(John 14:6) exists for all people.[1] However, this is not the accepted opinion within all of Christendom, as many scholars hold to the theology of dual covenantalism. For example, J. Christiaan Beker, who was impacted by his experiences as a Dutch political prisoner during World War II,[2] considers dual covenantalism as the best answer to the salvation question. He is joined by such theologians as Clark Williamson, Sidney Hall, and Rosemary Radford Ruether who believe that God has one plan of redemption for Israel and another for the Gentiles. Therefore, and to begin to answer the question of dual covenantalism, this chapter will begin with an overview of the biblical concept of "covenant," then endeavor to answer the question by examining both sides of the dual covenantalism issue in relation to Rom 9:1–5, and conclude with a final evaluation of the question.

BRIEF OVERVIEW OF THE BIBLICAL CONCEPT OF COVENANT

The concept of covenant plays a significant role in God's relationship to humanity from the very beginning of the creation story (Gen 1:28–31). God continued to relate to mankind through a covenant concept when He renewed it with Noah after the flood (Gen 9:8–17). However, the focus of a covenant relationship between God and specific people groups began with Abraham (Gen 12, 15, 17). Therefore, this is where we will begin to examine the covenant concept.

"Covenant" (*berith*) can be defined as a "covenant," "compact," or "pact" between two parties.[3] The covenant relationship between God and Abraham related specifically to God's promise "to multiply" Abraham's seed, "give them the land of Canaan, and make them [Abraham's descendants] a blessing to the nations."[4] According to Weinfeld, this idea of the biblical covenant should not be considered necessarily a "mutual

---

1. This writer holds to a one-covenant position as well as a rejection of the concept of Replacement Theology. This theological error will be discussed in chapter 7.

2. Beker, *Suffering and Hope*, xi.

3. *Hebrew and English Lexicon of the Old Testament*, s. v. "*berith*." See also, Weinfeld, "*berith*," TDOT, 2:253–54; Davidson, "Covenant Ideology in Ancient Israel," 324. Davidson provides additional information as to the mysterious etymology of *berith*, including the possible origins coming from the Akkadian root concept of "clasp or fetter."

4. *Hebrew and English Lexicon of the Old Testament*, s.v. "*berith*."

agreement," but rather a "commitment confirmed by an oath."[5] In other words, the covenant between God and Abraham was not one of equal parties agreeing to mutual obligations and commitments. The Abrahamic covenant, as well as the corresponding covenants between the Israelites (Deuteronomy 28–32) and David (Psalm 89), is one in which the obligations fall to God, and the opportunities belong to the people of God.[6]

Therefore, an important question to be asked with regard to understanding the relationship between God and the Jewish people through the covenants of Abraham, Moses, and David is whether the covenant can be nullified by either one or both parties.[7] However, a more nuanced question, and one that deals with some of the dual covenant positions, is whether nuances of the pact can change, or be fulfilled in an "unexpected way," without affecting the overall tenor of the covenant agreement?[8] Therefore, the rest of the chapter will consider the relationship of the Jewish people to the Abrahamic covenant and the reality of Jesus' Messiahship. Ultimately, consideration will be given to Jesus' impact on the eternal reality of this covenant, which was agreed upon four thousand years ago.

---

5. Weinfeld, "*berith*," TDOT, 2:255–56. See also, Nicholson, *God and His People*, 96; McCarthy, *Old Testament Covenant*, 2–3; and Eichrodt, *Theology of the Old Testament*, 1:37–43. Eichrodt, while lessening the impact of the one-sided nature of God's covenant with Abraham, does acknowledge that the responsibilities are "most unequally distributed." Additionally, he defines the concept as illustrating: (1) "the factual nature of the divine revelation"; (2) "a clear divine will"; (3) creates an awareness of the lesser role of humanity in the covenant; (4) reality of the fact that God is intimately involved in humanity's history; and (5) because an omnipotent God is involved with humanity, nature cannot be worshipped.

6. Weinfeld, "*berith*," TDOT, 2:270–73; and McCarthy, *Old Testament Covenant*, 54–55. For an explanation of the concept of the corporate election of the Jewish people, see Abasciano, "Corporate Election in Romans 9," 353.

7. Sandmel, 138–39. An interesting observation is that a Jewish scholar actually believes that the covenant was revocable, even revocable at the behest or actions of the Jewish people.

8. Hillers, *Covenant*, 179, 182–83. Hillers sees a clear relationship regarding continuity between the book of Hebrews and the Mosaic Covenant, as opposed to the need to refer back to the Abrahamic covenant as evidenced in the book of Romans. However, Hiller sees this relationship to the various covenants as an indication that the covenants are not broken, but rather fulfilled and revealed to their "deepest meaning."

ARGUMENTATION FAVORING DUAL COVENANTALISM

The basic premise of dual covenantalism is that the faiths of Christianity and Judaism should be respected within their own practices and doctrinal tenets. Furthermore, dual covenantalism would affirm that truth and "self-understanding" are inviolable rights of each faith, and to promote Christianity as the only way to God the Father is to deny the integrity of Judaism.[9] Craig Blaising, an opponent of dual covenantalism, defines the concept as a doctrine that takes "its primary orientation not from the Bible but from modern pluralism," and views the theology as a response to the Holocaust and Christianity's guilt for the apathetic response taken to oppose Hitler's evil machinations.[10] The pain of the Holocaust is something that has been brought into focus to me personally, due to the number of personal friends who are either survivors or children of individuals who lived through such places as Auschwitz and Bergen-Belsen. However, the question, which will be answered in the final summation section of this chapter, is whether the horrors of the Shoah allow for a dual-covenantal perspective.

The theology of dual covenantalism begins with an attempt to either deemphasize or lessen the reality of Paul's heartbreak in Romans 9:3. Krister Stendahl begins this approach by discounting Paul's encounter on the Damascus Road from one of conversion to simply a "special calling."[11] A second approach is to view the covenant(s) as now universal, and one in which the Gentiles are included, but the Jewish people are not excluded simply for rejecting the reality of Jesus' Messiahship.[12] In light of the real-

---

9. Anderson, "Re-reading Paul," Internet; Wasserberg, "Romans 9–11 and Jewish-Christian Dialogue," 176; Willimon, "Jews and Christians," 125; and van Buren, "Problem of a Christian Theology," 48. See also, Fisher, *Faith without Prejudice*, 83. Fisher follows the general approach of Anderson, but focuses upon the uniqueness of Judaism as proof of God's eternal promises to the nation of Israel.

10. Blaising, "Future of Israel," 440–41. Proof that the Holocaust is a probable cause for dual covenantalism can be seen in these words from Gregory Baum, "the churches have become aware that asking the Jews to become Christians is a spiritual way of blotting them out of existence and thus only reinforces the effects of the Holocaust." Baum, "Rethinking the Church's Mission," 113. See also, Cargas, "Christian Preaching after the Holocaust," 48–49.

11. Stendahl, *Paul Among Jews and Gentiles*, 7. Stendahl reflects that perhaps the question of Romans 9–11 "is the relation between two communities and their coexistence in the mysterious plan of God" (4).

12. Burghardt, "Response to Rosemary Ruether," 94–95; Fasching, *Narrative Theology After Auschwitz*, 34–35; Young, *Paul the Jewish Theologian*, 28, 32, 46, 138; and Stendahl, *Final Account*, 40–44.

Rationale and Error of Dual Covenantalism

ity that Gentiles are included into the promises of God through the surrender of Jesus on the cross, this approach is worthy of consideration; however, this approach should not be given credence at the expense of Jesus' sacrifice for both Jews and Gentiles. This tendency to make exceptions regarding the reality of Jesus' gift of salvation is one of the many failings of dual covenantalism. This approach of "picking-and-choosing" what to believe and what to discount creates a scriptural vacuum for dual covenantalism and results in the perception that nothing can be trusted.

Eugene Fisher elaborates on the fine points of dual covenantalism by spelling out particular aspects of the theology. Dual covenantalism does not believe that Jesus Christ has replaced the Jewish covenant of Mount Sinai, but instead "merely extends the one invitation to others."[13] He elucidates his view with the following positions: "(1) the Jewish covenant remains valid after Christ; (2) the Christian covenant is rooted in the ongoing reality of the Sinai covenant as its living source; and (3) stripped of its relationship with a living Judaism, Christianity would soon cease to exist."[14]

Rosemary Radford Ruether builds upon Fisher's premises and expands them to include two additional possibilities. The first is that God had no intention of saving the Jewish people through the Torah, which would therefore make Yahweh a monster for this false covenant. The second is that Jesus is not yet the Messiah, because it would deflect the validity of Judaism's story of redemption.[15] While both views are incorrect, Fisher's flawed approach at least attempts to approach the whole question from a theological perspective, whereas Ruether deals mainly in the speculative, non-theological world of hypothesis.

Of note is that, while ultimately holding to a position which allows the Jewish people to enter heaven without believing in Christ Jesus, some

---

13. Fisher, *Faith Without Prejudice*, 86; and Gaston, "Israel's Missteps in the Eyes of Paul," 315.

14. Fisher, *Faith Without Prejudice*, 87. See also, Baum, "Rethinking the Church's Mission," 127; Williamson and Allen, "Interpreting Difficult Texts," 40–41; Williamson, *Guest in the House of Israel*, 249; and Schwier, "Church and Israel," Internet.

15. Ruether, *Faith and Fratricide*, 106–7; and Holwerda, *Jesus and Israel*, 15. Gager, *Origins of Anti-Semitism*, 200–201, builds upon Ruether's argument when he writes that Jesus was only "the fulfillment of God's promises concerning the Gentiles." In other words, Gager's argument is that Jesus' Messiahship was limited to people with whom He had only limited encounters during His earthly ministry with no redemptive power for His own ethnic brothers and sisters.

theologians struggle with the concept of a classic dual covenantalism that is from the mold of Gager, Williamson, Ruether, Stendahl, and Gaston. E. P. Sanders writes that "it is God who will see to it that all Israel is saved, though this does not happen apart from Christ."[16] Sanders's premise creates an impossible theological dichotomy, which can border on religious schizophrenia due to the fact that he allows Jewish people to be saved through Jesus, even while affirming their right to refuse to believe in Him. Sanders himself acknowledges this inconsistency by stating that his view is "better asserted than explained,"[17] even while trying to blame his own problems at the feet of the "confusing" statements of Paul.

Günter Wasserberg would deny the accusation of schizophrenia, but can only resolve his own internal tension to the entire issue by placing the ultimate blame on Paul and the "deficient religion" expressed in the New Testament.[18] Sanders and Wasserberg should be given credit for attempting to hold to a more exegetical approach regarding the eternal condition of the Jewish people. However, they ultimately choose to follow, albeit in a more approachable manner to evangelical Christians,[19] classic dual covenantalism. This consent to dual covenantalism ultimately is detrimental to the eternal condition of the Jewish people,[20] regardless of their good intentions. The danger of good intentions is that it is a path destined for eternal separation in hell.

ARGUMENTATION OPPOSING DUAL COVENANTALISM

Dual covenantalism is flawed, and presents an alternative to the Messianic plan of redemption that is contrary to Scripture. As noted previously,

16. Sanders, *Paul, the Law, and the Jewish People*, 194–95, 197.
17. Sanders, *Paul, the Law, and the Jewish People*, 198.
18. Wasserberg, "Romans 9–11 and Jewish-Christian Dialogue," 184–85.

19. This approachable manner has attracted a select, but growing number of evangelical Christian leaders, including John Hagee, who will be considered in more detail in the summation section.

20. Dual Covenantalists often react strongly to any attempt to share the Gospel (what they would call conversion techniques) with the Jewish people. See Alston, "Root that Supports Us," 105–7. Williamson, *Guest in the House of Israel*, 243–45, 250–52, and van Buren, "Problem of a Christian Theology," 62–64, devotes considerable time to justifying the "Jewish No" to the Christian message, primarily because the horrors of the Holocaust create a situation that invalidates any message of Jesus' love. While on the surface this approach is palatable to Christian guilt, it does nothing to eliminate the reality of the eternal destiny of the Jewish people who do not receive the truth of Jesus' Messiahship.

Blaising believes that dual covenantalism owes its support to the fallacy of "modern pluralism." Additionally, he considers the view that Christianity and Judaism are "validly separate religions" to be an affront to "both Christianity and Judaism at their fundamental, that is Biblical, levels."[21]

Blaising's indictment of the possibility of two unique religious approaches to God requires one to consider the ultimate motivation of certain theologians and organizations, such as the World Council of Churches. The rationale for seeking an alternative destiny for the Jewish people who deny the Messiahship of Jesus can most likely be found in the ovens of Auschwitz. However, to seek such an alternative is not only an attempt to revise two thousand years of Christian history but also, and most importantly, is an effort to change the emphasis of the New Testament itself.[22]

James D. G. Dunn sums up the opposition to dual covenantalism when he surmises "that the new covenant is best understood as a renewal of the old."[23] However, one must be careful to understand that, while Dunn is correct in his view of a covenant renewal (cf. Jer 31:31–34), he walks a fine line of including Jewish people into the new covenant without requiring them to affirm their faith in Jesus Christ.[24] This tendency of apparent inclusion, without a faith commitment, is something of which all opponents of dual covenantalism must be careful when they address the subject.[25] One must understood that a faith commitment in Jesus is

---

21. Blaising, "Future of Israel," 441. Blaising debunks not only the Jewish argument, but also the Dual Covenant argument of Rosemary Radford Ruether that Jesus could not be the Messiah, because He did not bring in the Messianic Age. He focuses in on the "already-but-not-yet" aspect of the kingdom of God as his focus of debating the point against Rabbinic Judaism and a possible dual covenantal perspective (442).

22. Holwerda, *Jesus and Israel*, 19; and Johnson, "Romans 9–11," 213–14. One can read Johnson as desiring a point for which to disprove Pauline thought concerning the lost condition of the Jewish people; however, she is left with no alternative but to agree with Paul's position. She writes, "Paul is more confident about his grasp of things eternal than most moderns are of their handle on things temporal."

23. Dunn, "Judaism and Christianity," 53.

24. Dunn, "Judaism and Christianity," 54.

25. Even vehement opponents to Replacement Theology (supersessionism) can find themselves submitting to this dangerous theological trap. R. Kendall Soulen states that "to be a Gentile means to be the other of Israel and as such a full participant in a single economy of mutual blessings anchored in God's carnal election of the Jewish people." This statement might not seem to fall into the trap until one considers additional comments, "But the church, above all in its gentile portion, should cease organized mission

required by everyone from every race and nation, regardless of one's previous relationship with God. This worldwide salvation commitment is for all peoples and can be called "God's grand salvific plan."[26]

In addition, and as mentioned previously, the reality is that nuances of the Abrahamic covenant changed and were fulfilled in an "unexpected way" through Messiah Jesus. However, the overall tenor of the covenant agreement was not changed from when the promises were first given to Abraham, Moses, and David. This truth is understood and begrudgingly accepted by even some prominent contemporary Jewish scholars, including Dan Cohn-Sherbok.[27] The reality of Rom 9:1–5, and the entirety of chapters 9–11, illustrate that Paul had a personal and ethnic stake regarding the Jewish people. He could not have expressed such grief if the possibility existed that they could be redeemed apart from Christ. His ethnic heritage and apostolic mission were evidenced in this passage describing a grief that reached to the depths of Paul's soul.[28]

SUMMATION ON DUAL COVENANTALISM

Dual covenantalism has been shown to be flawed on a basic theological level. Dual-covenant scholars follow theological principles that require a case of religious schizophrenia, as is the case of E. P. Sanders and Günter Wasserberg or Rosemary Radford Ruether's "blasphemous" rejection of Jesus' claim of divinity. One simply cannot follow dual covenantalism and hold to the integrity of Scripture.

However, the greatest danger of dual covenantalism does not lie in the minds of liberal theologians. The danger lies in how this path can lead evangelical Christians into a morass of apathy regarding the souls of the Jewish people. Prominent, albeit controversial, evangelical John Hagee is

---

efforts among the Jewish people. Instead the church of the Gentiles should seek to live before the Jewish people in such a way that Israel can reasonably infer that here the nations of the world truly worship the God of Israel and in this way manifests the truth of the gospel (see Rom 11:13–14)." Soulen, *God of Israel*, 130, 173.

26. Kim, *God, Israel, and the Gentiles*, 113.

27. Cohn-Sherbok, *Crucified Jew*, 20. Cohn-Sherbok does not attempt to hide his resentment of this biblical approach, even while incorrectly diagnosing it as proof of both Replacement Theology and Dual Covenantalism. He writes, "Since Jews and gentiles belong to fallen humanity as represented by the Old Adam, salvation can only come through a new covenant based on Christ."

28. Wright, *Climax of the Covenant*, 237.

one example of how the path to dual covenantalism is very short if one is not careful to guard one's theological principles. In his work *Jerusalem Countdown*, John Hagee attempts to walk the fine line of acceptability within the larger religious community, while maintaining his conservative, fundamentalist credentials.[29] For example, he implies that repentance of sins for the Jewish people is guaranteed through the yearly observance of Yom Kippur, that Jewish people are saved only through "divine revelation," and that de-emphasizing Paul's willingness for perdition is acceptable if it would save the ethnic Jewish race.[30]

This downward progression against the call for Jewish evangelism will not necessarily lead an evangelical into the arms of liberalism. The real danger is in how it might affect the worldwide approach to evangelism. If "to the Jew first" is neglected, then can "and also the Gentiles," be far behind? The previous statement could be dismissed as fear-mongering until one considers the words of Cohn-Sherbok:

> Such a reorientation of Christian mission is based on the recognition of God's presence in all the world's religious faiths—a view which is increasingly accepted by many Christians. This shift in perspective is grounded in the conviction that a God of love could not allow the mass of humanity to wallow in ignorance and darkness: as the providential Lord of history, God must provide a means of salvation for all people.[31]

Unfortunately, Cohn-Sherbok and others fail to realize that God did provide a "means of salvation for all people [Jew and Gentile alike]," and His name is Jesus. Thus, regardless of the discomfort created by worldwide church apathy during the Holocaust,[32] or the basic human emotion to find

---

29. Hagee, *Jerusalem Countdown*. No page number is referenced, as the book in its entirety is devoted to the issue at hand.

30. Hagee, *Jerusalem Countdown*, 129, 174–75.

31. Cohn-Sherbok, *Crucified Jew*, 230.

32. Downey, "Apologetic," 1–16. I was given the privilege this year to present a paper at the International Society of Christian Apologetics on the subject of Jewish evangelism in light of the Holocaust. The task was simultaneously a privilege and an onerous one, because for too long the liberal faction of Christendom has "guilted" the church into doing nothing about the salvation of the Jewish people, while the conservative faction has often reacted negatively to an implication that Christian apathy is a factor in the Holocaust. However, the truth is something we as Christians must confront and respond to with evangelistic fervor if we hope to see victory in the cause of Jewish evangelism. A complete copy of the paper can be viewed at http://www.isca-apologetics.org/node/226.

an alternative to eternal separation from God for His Chosen Ones, the truth is that just as Jack and Barbara Downey had one set of guidelines for their daughters, God has one set of guidelines for His Jewish and Gentile children—receiving Jesus as Messiah.

7

Argument of Replacement Theology (Romans 9:1–5)

ONE OF THE PRIVILEGES of graduating with two degrees from Southwestern Baptist Theological Seminary was the opportunity to learn from an amazing array of professors, such as Siegfried Schatzmann for Greek, Craig Blaising for Eschatology, and Calvin Miller for Christian Faith and the Arts, to name just a few. Additionally, I had the amazing privilege of working for John Newport and being called "Fair Lady" by a true Southern gentleman. Words fail me to describe the honor of assisting James Leo Garrett, as he completed volume two of his Systematic Theology *magnum opus*.

I was able to see a side to E. Earle Ellis that few saw, and even fewer could imagine. In his classes, the "Theology of Paul" and the "Theology of Jesus," Dr. Ellis conveyed a passion for his subject that belied his age. He acknowledged the continued need for the Jewish people to hear the Gospel message, despite his support of "Replacement Theology." This might surprise many, as replacement theology or supersessionism is the doctrinal view that God has rejected the Jews as His chosen people, due to the Jewish rejection of Jesus' Messiahship.[1] In fact, Dr. Ellis relayed that while he believed that the Church was the "New Israel," he still sent a monthly gift to Jews for Jesus so that the Jewish people might hear that Jesus was still for them.

---

1. Breidenthal, "Neighbor-Christology," 319; Holwerda, *Jesus and Israel*, 50; Horner, *Future Israel*, 78; and Bloesch, "All Israel Will be Saved," 130. Bloesch repeats a common refrain, and one that will be acknowledged in this chapter, that the Holocaust created a spiritual obstacle to replacement theology that is difficult for even the most ardent supporter to overcome. One should note that, while Bloesch opposes replacement theology, he is not an advocate of dual covenantalism.

Replacement theology[2] has been attacked as not only insensitive, but also indefensible in a post-Holocaust society, with the loudest voice of opposition coming from the liberal spectrum of Christianity.[3] While the theologically correct position is to join the chorus against a replacement theology which advocates that Judaism stands in complete opposition to Christianity,[4] the presumption that the answer must lie in the arguments of dual covenantalism would be equally irresponsible.[5] Thankfully, Dr. Ellis avoided dual covenantalism and supported a replacement theological viewpoint that included Jewish people in the evangelistic plan of God. However, and much as I respect him, E. Earle Ellis was wrong in this particular understanding of Scripture, as are so many in modern-day Christendom.

Therefore, a need exists to establish a beginning point for developing an evaluation of replacement theology. One could support Franklin Littell's argument that this doctrinal premise is simply a case of allegorical hermeneutics and anti-Semitic inclinations of reading impossible-to-prove concepts into the Old Testament.[6] An alternative position to my own personal view and that of Littell's view is to consider the fact that, while replacement theology is incorrect, the work of evangelical scholarship should focus on separating theology from the biases of history,[7] and seek to create a "Christian story" that strives for faithfulness to the original intent.[8] Therefore, this chapter will consider the historical premise of replacement theology, along with the arguments both in favor of and opposed to this theological premise. The chapter will then conclude with a summation of the argument and an evaluation of the entire issue, which will include a closing admonition from Dr. Ellis himself.

---

2. In order to avoid confusion, I have decided to utilize replacement theology as the common vernacular for this chapter.

3. Diprose, *Israel and the Church*, 30–31.

4. Baur, *Paul*, 182. Baur specifically considers Christianity to be a completely new διαθήκη (covenant or testament) from Judaism. Baur goes on to state that Christianity contains "a totally new principle of religious life."

5. Williamson and Allen, "Interpreting Difficult Texts," 40.

6. Littell, *Crucifixion of the Jews*, 28–29, 30–31; see also, Lohfink, *Covenant Never Revoked*, 87, 92.

7. Soulen, *God of Israel and Christian Theology*, 17.

8. Soulen, *God of Israel and Christian Theology*, 13.

HISTORY OF REPLACEMENT THEOLOGY

In evaluating the history of replacement theology, the first issue to be confronted is whether the historical evidence comes from the biblical text, or whether the biblical text was manipulated by the early Church fathers.[9] This matter can be answered by analyzing the positions of the early Church fathers to determine whether biblical passages or personal biases helped to formulate their support of replacement theology.[10]

The Epistle of Barnabas is perhaps the first letter to advocate a view that the church of God has replaced the Jewish nation as the people of God. The actual date for the writing of the epistle is in question, ranging from AD 96 to 130,[11] but the emphasis was two-fold: (1) comparing the old (Jews) and the new (the church) people of God and (2) blaming the Jewish people for the death of Jesus.[12] The division of the covenant into the new and old people of God, according to the epistle of Barnabas, did not begin at the cross, but at Mount Sinai as the anonymous author believed that the Jewish people never took ownership of the promises that were offered to them.[13]

If the Epistle of Barnabas is the first (albeit non-canonical) letter promoting replacement theology to the churches, Ignatius of Antioch (AD 114) is the first church father to advocate replacement theology.[14] Mark Kinzer believes that Ignatius is the first church father to promote

---

9. Shimkus, "*Adversus Ioudaeos*," 2. Shimkus considers the historical events of the time to have influenced the Church fathers. However, Shimkus does allow that the polemical message of the Gospels played a contributing factor in influencing the Patristic theologians to begin to advocate replacement theology. The possibility of a polemical message of the Gospel is a debate worth discussing, but not necessarily in the context of this book.

10. Due to the scope of Patristic history and basic page limitations, only a brief analysis of the subject is possible.

11. Wilson, *Related Strangers*, 126–27, 139; and Kinzer, *Postmissionary Messianic Judaism*, 189–91. Wilson prefers the earliest date possible, while Kinzer supports a date just prior to the Bar Kokhba rebellion of AD 135.

12. Wilson, *Related Strangers*, 128–29.

13. Wilson, *Related Strangers*, 136–38. Wilson, in analyzing the Barnabas epistle, considers Romans 9—11 as something of an aberration in comparison to all the canonical and non-canonical epistles. This writer disagrees with Wilson, but his premise is an acknowledgement that to read replacement theology into Rom 9:1–5 specifically is dubious at best.

14. Kinzer, *Postmissionary Messianic Judaism*, 187–89; and Hann, "Supersessionism, Engraftment, and Jewish-Christian Dialogue," 331–32.

the concept that Judaism and Christianity are "two separate religious systems," and that Jewish Christians should be admonished for maintaining any traditional Jewish observances.[15] In the late second century, Justin Martyr became the next prominent church father to teach that God had ceased to be concerned with the fate of the Jewish people. His *Dialogue with Trypho* (AD 155–160) was based upon a supposed conversation with a Jewish man Trypho,[16] whom Justin tried to convert to Christianity. One of his arguments is that, while the Old Testament should not be viewed allegorically, it should be considered as an antitype to the reality of Christ and the New Testament.[17]

Church history and the relationship with Judaism took an ominous turn with the conversion of Constantine (AD 313) and the official recognition of Christianity in AD 380 under Theodosius.[18] This period opened the door to increasing verbal diatribes and physical assaults against the Jewish people.[19] In my opinion, the preeminent preacher and main instigator of both replacement theology and anti-Semitic tirades is John Chrysostom (347–407).[20] Chrysostom's invective was built upon the premise that the

---

15. Kinzer, *Postmissionary Messianic Judaism*, 185–86.

16. Kinzer, *Postmissionary Messianic Judaism*, 191–94. While the existence of Trypho is questionable, Kinzer reports that, according to Justin Martyr, Trypho was a refugee from the Bar Kokhba rebellion in AD 135.

17. Soulen, *God of Israel and Christian Theology*, 38; and Wilson, *Related Strangers*, 89, 90, 93. Justin himself stated in the conclusion of his dialogue with Trypho, "There is no other way than this, that you come to know *our* [writer's emphasis] Christ, be baptized with the baptism which cleanses you of sin (as Isaiah testified), and thus live a life free of sin." Martyr, "Dialogue with Trypho," 99.

18. Fasching, *Narrative Theology after Auschwitz*, 18.

19. Fasching, *Narrative Theology after Auschwitz*, 18.

20. Wilson, *Our Father Abraham*, 95; and Fasching, *Narrative Theology after Auschwitz*, 19.

Jewish people are "Christ-killers,"[21] that their crime results in the hatred of God toward them, and that forgiveness is impossible.[22]

The church fathers were able to turn toward replacement theology due to the hermeneutical approach of allegory. Through this approach, Wilson believes that allegory allowed the church fathers to make the Old Testament a Christian document.[23] Aphrahat, bishop of Mar Mattai, utilized Old Testament allegorization to show that the Jewish people had been replaced as the chosen people.[24] In the fifth century, Augustine of Hippo took the premise of allegorization to the highest level and found that the purpose of the Jews had been reduced simply to a reminder of what happens when someone rejects Jesus as Messiah—they will be replaced and doomed to perdition.[25] Perhaps Cyril of Alexandria best illustrates the use of allegory in connection with Romans 9:1–5 when he describes the Jews as "rejected and abandoned and excluded from God's company, placed behind even the Gentiles and cut off from the hope promised to the ancestors."[26]

A great debt is owed to the early church fathers for persevering for the faith in the face of Roman opposition to the Gospel message. However, their dependence upon allegory and personal biases has created a modern theological situation in which the presumption exists that one is either a dual covenantalist or a proponent of replacement theology.

---

21. Wilson, *Our Father Abraham*, 95; and Meeks and Wilken, *Jews and Christians in Antioch*, 87, 90. Meeks and Wilken provide a translation of Chrysostom's *Homilia Adversus Judaeos* for illustration purposes. Through this translation, the reader can begin to develop an understanding of Chrysostom's attitude toward the Jewish people. "Do not be surprised if I have called the Jews wretched. They are truly wretched and miserable for they have received many good things from God yet they have spurned them and violently cast them away.... This is why they are wretched, because when others embraced and welcomed the good things given to them, the Jews refused them.... They were called to sonship, but they degenerated to the level of dogs.... If they are ignorant of the Father, if they crucified the son, and spurned the aid of the Spirit, can one not declare with confidence that the synagogue is a dwelling place of demons? God is not worshipped there. Far from it! Rather the synagogue is a temple of idolatry."

22. Fasching, *Narrative Theology after Auschwitz*, 19.

23. Wilson, *Our Father Abraham*, 97; see also, Blaising, "Future of Israel as a Theological Question," 436–37.

24. Aphrahat, "On the Peoples Which are in the Place of the People," 21–25.

25. Carmichael, *Satanizing of the Jews*, 36–37; Augustine, "Reply to Faustus the Manichean," 30; and Diprose, *Israel and the Church*, 160–67.

26. Bray, *Romans*, 247; see also, Corley, "Significance of Romans 9–11," 42–43.

This theological quandary necessitates an approach, which recognizes the continuing position of the Jewish people in the Abrahamic covenant, but acknowledges that these same covenant people also need to receive Jesus as Messiah. Douglas Moo describes it as understanding the Jews "from the perspective of salvation history" and "their relationship to God and his promises to them."[27] I would describe it as God's people needing Messiah Jesus, for even though the Abrahamic covenant exists in perpetuity, the new covenant of Jeremiah 31 offers the plan for eternity.

ARGUMENTS RELATED TO REPLACEMENT THEOLOGY

One of the primary issues to be considered in evaluating the validity of replacement theology is whether or not biblical covenants, especially the ones instituted by God, can be dissolved[28] or reconstituted to reflect a position that was not evident in the initial "negotiations" of the agreement. Advocates of replacement theology often point to the reality of the Messiahship of Jesus as evidence that the covenant had been reconfigured to be something that was unexpected and unanticipated.[29] F. C. Baur is one example of a replacement theologian who affirmed this position. He stated that Judaism is not just a "negative relation to Christianity" but is, in fact, the exact opposite to the "grace of Christianity."[30]

Another approach, and one that is less inflammatory than Baur's in support of the replacement theology position, is to focus on the blessings provided to Gentiles, while affirming that these blessings create a deficit for the Jews.[31] However, and regardless of which replacement

27. Moo, *Epistle to the Romans*, 561.

28. Jones and Tarwater, "Are Biblical Covenants Dissoluble?" 1–11, esp. 8–11. The purpose of this article is primarily the issue of marriage covenants. However, Jones and Tarwater note that a covenant in which God plays a role is a covenant that should be considered as to be without an expiration date—in other words eternal.

29. Campbell, *Israel and the New Covenant*, 14–15, 125; Aagaard, "Church and the Jews in Eschatology," 273–74; Hillers, *Covenant*, 179, 182–83; Johnson, *Reading Romans*, 149; and Cohn-Sherbok. *Crucified Jew*, 20. Cohn-Sherbok serves as a Reformed rabbi, but affirms the position that Christianity and the New Testament advocate replacement theology.

30. Baur, *Paul*, 191. Baur, 210–11, acknowledges the special distinction of Judaism, as opposed to the heathen practices of the Canaanites. However, his ultimate comparison of Judaism to be the antitype of Christianity illustrates his negative perception of the teachings of Old Testament Judaism.

31. Holwerda, *Jesus and Israel*, 158; Rowley, *Biblical Doctrine of Election*, 149; Klein, *New Chosen People*, 20–21, 258. While arguing for a reconfiguration understanding of the covenant relationship, Klein allows for the possibility that, while the "national or ethnic"

theology approach is taken, the Jewish understanding of "covenant reconfiguration" is to see it as a form of "spiritual genocide" —a genocide designed by Christianity to destroy the bonds that the Jewish people share with God.[32]

The initial response to this perception is to deny Jewish claims. However, the question that must be asked is whether the New Testament itself, or the theological understandings gleaned from the biblical texts, support a replacement theology position that is nothing more than the "spiritual genocide" of the Jewish people,[33] for you must understand that this is the understanding of the Jewish people. An adequate answer to this conundrum will enable Christian scholarship to respond in a way that affirms the uniqueness, specifically the exclusiveness, of Jesus' gracious gift of salvation, while negating the accusation of "spiritual genocide."

An adequate answer cannot be found until one considers the strengths and weaknesses of the replacement theology argument, especially as it relates to Rom 9:1–5 specifically and chapters 9–11 generally. One argument is that "Israel" should not be considered the Jewish people, but actually the "New Israel," which is the church.[34] Thomas Schreiner does not support the view that these verses refer to the Church, and believes that the verses, specifically 9:1–5, reveal Paul's heartache with regard to the lostness of the Jewish people.[35] However, he does infer that while 9:1–5 relates to ethnic Israel, the promises found in verses 4–5 belong to all believers (especially Gentile) as well.[36]

---

covenant is still intact, the spiritual connection is lost. On the surface, this position seems to allow for a resolution to the dynamic struggle between replacement theology and dual covenantalism. However, he withdraws from this position when he writes that "the Christian church now enjoys the *unique* [writer's emphasis] position of 'chosen people.'"

32. Fasching, *Narrative Theology after Auschwitz*, 21.

33. Breidenthal, "Neighbor-Christology," 320–21, 323, 341.

34. Corley, "Significance of Romans 9–11," 44. Bruce Corley does not necessarily agree with this assessment. However, he does support the possibility by his citation of C. F. D. Moule's position, "yet the fact remains that God's Israel, true Israel, was so radically different from what counted as Israel in the contemporary world, that there is an undeniable sense in which it is 'new.'" Moule, *Birth of the New Testament*, 39.

35. Schreiner, "Corporate and Individual Election," 374; and Schreiner, "Does Romans 9 Teach Individual Election unto Salvation," 27, 30.

36. Schreiner, "Does Romans 9 Teach Individual Election unto Salvation," 27, 30; and Schreiner, "Corporate and Individual Election," 373–75. Schreiner specifically calls for joint ownership of such blessings as "adoption" and "glory." See also, Wagner, *Heralds of the Good News*, 45; Siker, *Disinheriting the Jews*, 64–65, 67–68; Moo, *Epistle to the Romans*,

While an advocate of this position, Luke Timothy Johnson recognizes the problematic position in which this places Paul with regard to Rom 9:1–5. Johnson believes that if one affirms the idea that Gentiles have commandeered or been incorporated into the blessings of verses 4–5, this leads Paul to being forced to warn the Gentiles against the sin of pride (11:11–24) and to answer the charge that the Torah was insufficient.[37] Further, this problematic position creates a vacuum and distance between the two testaments. This vacuum causes many churches and Christian scholars to lose the essence and basic meaning of the Old Testament stories, prophecies, and promises.[38] For instance, I once had a New Testament scholar ask me if Jesus really celebrated Hanukkah (John 10:22–31)!

Therefore, if ethnic Israel was merely a secondary plan in the overall schema of God's design for the world, then one might ask what was God's purpose for humanity from Abraham to the time of Jesus? Additionally, replacement theology creates the question of why Paul was lamenting the eternal destiny of the Jewish people in verses 1–3.[39] This core problem with replacement theology cannot be resolved by affirming this theological doctrine, because by doing so, one is left with far more questions than answers.

Ultimately, it should be acknowledged that Israel has not been replaced by the Church.[40] The original covenants, whether Abrahamic,

---

549; Chae, *Paul as Apostle to the Gentiles*, 225; and Freudmann, *Antisemitism in the New Testament*, 112. It should be noted that Freudmann is a Jewish scholar who, in her writings, appears to be determined to find anti-Semitic leanings in the New Testament, as evidenced by the title of her book. However, Freudmann's position of the Jewish blessings being commandeered by the Gentiles finds support in Christian theology, even though those same Christian scholars would deny the charge of anti-Semitism. Wright, *Climax of the Covenant*, 237, expresses a dichotomous position in regard to this issue. While he affirms the concept of the privileges, especially chapters 5–8, he asserts that the privileges described in Rom 9:1–5 belong solely to the Jewish people.

37. Johnson, *Reading Romans*, 158. See also, Witherington, *Paul's Letter to the Romans*, 245.

38. Soulen, *God of Israel and Christian Theology*, 12.

39. Kim, *God, Israel, and the Gentiles*, 101, 113. Kim understands Paul's lament to be "a strong statement that the salvation of the Jewish people is not alien to his ministry but is at the core of it."

40. Blaising, "Future of Israel as a Theological Question," 437; and Diprose, *Israel and the Church*, 54–57. Diprose notes various scholars who recognize the uniqueness of Israel's election, while maintaining the extension of those benefits to Gentiles. Diprose

Argument of Replacement Theology

Mosaic, or Davidic, are still in existence. Israel has the rights and privileges of the covenant that was ultimately fulfilled in Jesus of Nazareth. However, and unlike the view of dual covenantalism, they must both recognize and receive Jesus' Messiahship in order to receive the full benefits of the covenant.[41] This desperate longing that the Jewish people will receive the truth of the Gospel message is the anguish of Paul's soul, because it should be acknowledged that while Israel is "in crisis," Israel "is still Israel."[42] The Jewish people (Israel) need the cross of Christ as does the rest of humanity. The cross should never create an environment of "spiritual genocide" for the Jewish people or any people group.[43] The cross is the only preventive measure that can overcome the dangers of eternal damnation for the Jew and the Gentile. This is the point of Romans 9:1–5 and the reason for Paul's anguish and desperate prayer for the salvation of the Jewish people.

SUMMATION ON REPLACEMENT THEOLOGY

If dual covenantalism is the religiously correct option in today's multi-religious society, replacement theology is considered the incorrect and insensitive approach to resolving the question regarding the place of the Jews in the overall salvation plan for the world. However, neither approach ultimately solves the problem of what might be the eternal destiny of those Jewish people who reject and deny the Messiahship of Jesus. However, it should be acknowledged that replacement theology at least considers and acknowledges the problem. Donald Bloesch considers replacement theology to be guilty of "triumphalism," but dual covenantalism to be nothing more than "syncretism," which denigrates "the uniqueness of the Christ revelation."[44]

---

ultimately rejects this position and affirms that the Israel of Romans 9:1–5 refers only to ethnic Israel.

41. Bloesch, "All Israel Will be Saved," 132.

42. Horner, *Future Israel*, 309; and Kinzer, *Postmissionary Messianic Judaism*, 124–25, 130–31. A contrary position to Kinzer's statement is elucidated by Ben Witherington, *Paul's Letter to the Romans*, 250. Witherington believes that 9:4, with corollary evidence in verse six, shows that not all Jewish people are Jews in the eyes of God.

43. Soulen, *God of Israel and Christian Theology*, 168. Soulen specifically writes, "The cross has nothing whatever to do with the denial or destruction of Israel's national privilege." In this statement and corresponding sentences, Soulen affirms the truth that Messiah Jesus brings ultimate fulfillment of the covenant to the Jewish people.

44. Bloesch, "All Israel Will be Saved," 138.

Aside from the charges of "spiritual genocide" and anti-Semitism facing replacement theology, the theological arguments are lacking in strength and consistency. The contradictions begin with the theologians who debate the issue of whether the Israelites in Rom 9:1–5 should be considered as the Church of God, as opposed to the original people of God. This approach and divergence of opinions creates a spiritual disconnect between the Old and New Testaments[45] and/or forces biblical scholars to resort to the early church fathers' approach of allegorical hermeneutics. Replacement theology, despite the problems, does acknowledge the ultimate need for everyone, including the Jewish people, to receive Jesus as Messiah and Lord.[46] Therefore, if one is to err, the preferred error would be on the side of replacement theology. However, the best option is to negate both errors and go with the truth.

The solution to defining a middle approach, which affirms the continuation of ethnic Israel's place in the covenant, without sacrificing the uniqueness and exclusivity of Christ's death and resurrection, cannot be resolved in the pages of this book. However, the work of resolving this quandary should begin here. It is not enough that evangelical Christians, the primary group that struggles with the issue of replacement theology, are considered to be greater friends to the nation of Israel.[47] Can friendship be true if we do not proclaim that the Jewish people must receive Jesus in order to receive eternal life and the ultimate blessings of the covenant? Consequently, replacement theology versus dual covenantalism is not the primary issue, even though a proper understanding of each is essential to developing a mission mindset toward the Jewish people. The primary issue should be the need to share the Gospel message to those

---

45. Soulen, *God of Israel and Christian Theology*, 32–33.

46. Soulen, *God of Israel and Christian Theology*, 139; and Campbell, *Israel and the New Covenant*, 23. Roderick Campbell, who should never be considered as anything but a replacement theologian, states quite categorically that "the task of the Christian is to win the world, including the Jew, to the faith of the Messiah who has already come." See also, Breidenthal, "Neighbor-Christology," 322. Breidenthal provides a unique twist to the situation and considers dual covenantalism in its own way to be a form of replacement theology. In his criticism of "inclusivity," he considers this need to allow all peoples into heaven, regardless of their belief systems, to be a replacement of the exclusive claims of Christianity.

47. Littell, *Crucifixion of the Jews*, 33. As a scholar who would not be considered evangelical, this appears to be a difficult admission for Littell to make. He also, and perhaps correctly, considers the friendship of many evangelical Christians to be "provisional" and related to dispensationalism's desire to hasten the return of the Lord.

for whom it was first intended, and they were—and remain—the Jewish people, the Chosen People of God.[48]

For too long, this Christian undertaking has forgotten the anguished lament of Paul who was willing to forsake the blessings of eternity with Christ for the salvation of the Jewish people (Rom 9:3). The twenty-first-century Church must forsake the religiously correct comfort zone of apathy and ineptitude, and include the people of the covenant into the reality of the covenant promises.[49]

I began this chapter with an allusion to sitting under the teaching of E. Earle Ellis, a replacement theologian who was burdened for the salvation of the Jewish people to the point that he was a monthly contributor to Jews for Jesus. I took away from his classes, even while disagreeing with his replacement position, that salvation is a gift that must be shared with the world . . . and shared now. Additionally, I would like to add that, like Paul and his lament of Rom 9:1–5, we must first begin with the Chosen Ones of God.

---

48. Bloesch, "All Israel Will be Saved," 140–41.
49. Diprose, *Israel and the Church*, 189.

Conclusion

THE OVERALL PURPOSE OF this book has been to examine Paul's relationship with his own Jewish people through an exegetical and theological examination of two passages, 1 Thess 2:13–16 and Rom 9:1–5. The intention was to show that the two passages, which appear on the surface to be contradictory, actually reveal a unified passion to see the Jewish people come to faith in Messiah Jesus.

Paul was not an anti-Semite. Paul was not a self-hating Jew. The churches at Rome and Thessalonica were drastically different. The church of Thessalonica had a limited number of Jewish believers. The Roman church not only had a substantial Jewish membership, especially after the Claudian expulsion was revoked by Nero, but also the founding members of the church were, in fact, Jewish. This fact alone provides one possible clue for why the tone and approach of Paul to the two churches was so different. He was speaking to his audience, not expecting his audience to adapt to him. This understanding is one of the first things I teach my students at Arlington Baptist College where I presently am a professor of General Studies. Know your people and speak to them.

Paul was a student of Scripture. As a Pharisee and student of Gamaliel, he knew the Torah. He knew the prophecies of the Tanakh (i.e., Old Testament). Additionally, as we all know, he is responsible for most of our New Testament. Therefore, when we look at his apparently vitriolic reaction to the Jews of 1 Thess 2:13–16, we must look at it through his Jewish eyes. Then we can see that it is not in contradiction to his anguish and lament over the spiritual depravity of the Jewish people.

Hopefully, this work has shown you that despite his indictment of the "the Jews" (των Ἰουδαίων) for their actions, the people of his anger were not wholly or completely the people of his ethnicity. These "Jews" were accused of killing the Lord Jesus (των καὶ τὸν κύριον ἀποκτειν-άντων Ἰησουν) and, consequently, the prophets of the Lord. The punishment for this offense, and one that involves a great deal of controversy, is whether the wrath of God "to the utmost" involves all Jewish people (i.e., all Jewish people for all time are damned for their rejection of Jesus), or only those who reject the message of the Gospel. This book's position is to show the reader that it only refers to those who reject the Gospel and attempt to deny others from hearing this message of hope. Consequently, the Thessalonian chapter came to the conclusion that Paul's reaction, which admittedly is full of anger and recrimination, is not anti-Semitic, but rather is compatible with the Jewish approach to a polemical in-house debate.[1]

In many ways, the chapter examination of the Romans passage in one way is much easier to digest, and in another way is more heartbreaking. The Romans passage focused on two primary issues: (1) the depth of anguish of Paul's heart was so great that he would have given up heaven, salvation, and Jesus if it would mean that the Jewish people would come to faith; and (2) the reality that the passage in question is referring to the blessings of the Jewish nation and not a replacement position in which the Church is now considered as Israel.

The depth of Paul's anguish is illustrated by his oath in which he swears not only by his own word, but also through the testimony of Jesus and the Holy Spirit. This expression provides extra credence to his statement that he would be willing (wishing/praying) to face hell itself if it would mean the salvation of the Jewish people.

The reality of those for whom Paul was willing to face damnation is understood by the terminology of his kinsmen after the flesh who are Israelites, ὑπὲρ των ἀδελφων μου των συγγενων μου κατὰ σάρκα ανδ οἵτινὲ εἰσιν Ἰσραηλιται. This section of the book sought to bring to light the reality that the Jewish people had been given great gifts that were being lost because of their rejection of Jesus' Messiahship. In verses 4–5, the true and glorious fulfillment of these promises belongs to the Jewish people, but will not be realized if Jesus does not become the savior of their hearts.

The final three chapters focused on theological controversies that are a result of these two passages. The first controversy related specifically to the issue of whether the words of 1 Thess 2:13–16 are actually the words

---

1. See page XX of chapter 3, and Hagner, "Paul's Quarrel with Judaism," 134; Dodd, *Problem with Paul*, 119–20; Holmes, *1 and 2 Thessalonians*, 86–87; Wanamaker, *Epistles to the Thessalonians*, 118; Holtz, "Judgment on the Jews and the Salvation of All Israel," 285–86; and Ellis, *Pauline Theology*, 132–33.

of Paul. Many desire to declare that either Paul was an anti-Semite, or that these words were not from Paul's own hand. Chapter 5 presents the arguments of those who support the concept of interpolation, and determined that—while it might solve the problem one faces—upon a surface examination of the Thessalonian passage, it is an incorrect assumption to view this passage as being anything but Pauline in nature and scope.

In many ways, defending Pauline authorship was easier to reconcile than the false twin assumptions generated by Rom 9:1–5 (chapters 6–7). Dual covenantalism is comfortable, because it allows for the option that, while Gentiles are saved by the sacrifice of Jesus on the cross, Jewish people are redeemed through—and only through—the Old Testament covenants—dual covenantalism. The primary advocates of this position do appear to come from a more liberal theological position. Their position is appealing in a post-Holocaust world, and "answers" the anti-Semitic charges of 1 Thess 2:13–16. However, while appealing, this position causes only a sense of religious schizophrenia—a schizophrenia that does nothing but water down and cheapen Jesus' sacrifice and victory of the cross.

The third and final controversy examined was that of replacement theology. This is a theology that views the Church as now having replaced Israel as the chosen people of God. Credit was given, in one sense, to the idea of replacement theology, for it encourages an exclusive approach to salvation. However, the doctrine was ultimately rejected, because it fails to do an adequate job of avoiding the dangers of allegorical hermeneutics, and loses a sense of the importance of the original meaning of the Old Testament to the New Testament story.

Ultimately, the premise for this work was based upon my two-fold desire. The first aim is to express adequately from a theological and academic perspective an answer to those who downplay or deny the importance of Jewish evangelism.[2] The second aim is based upon the writer's heart for Jewish missions and a desire for those who promote this mission endeavor to approach it both from the heart and from a scholarly perspective, and not simply in a reactionary mode. To many in Christendom, the Messianic movement often appears to revolve around minutiae issues, such as the value of a Jewish believer keeping kosher, and not upon the

---

2. Diprose, *Israel and the Church*, 189; and Saperstein, *Moments of Crisis*, 61. As an unbelieving Jew, Saperstein is offended personally by the concept of Jewish evangelism/missions, but recognizes that, for Christians to deny the cause of Jewish missions, is to abandon the cause of evangelism in general.

heavier matters of Scripture. Truly, this is not the case for many Messianic scholars, but the assumption still needs to be disproved in order for serious consideration to be given in the "mainstream" of evangelical, conservative Christian scholarship.

My view is that if those involved in the Messianic movement and Jewish missions focus upon theological and exegetical concerns such as the interrelationship between 1 Thess 2:13–16 and Rom 9:1–5, the movement and work of Jewish evangelism would benefit from greater involvement by the Church as a whole. Many in the Messianic world will perhaps be offended by the last few sentences. However, I believe I am validated by the words of Hebrew Christian Jacob Jocz who believed that in order for Christianity to realize its purpose fully, it must recognize the importance of Jewish evangelism and missions.[3] Further, if the movement is not taken seriously, how can they recognize its importance?

The work of Jewish evangelism is not an easy endeavor, but neither is it optional. Christians and the Church must be about the work of reaching the ethnic brothers and sisters of Messiah Jesus with the Gospel. Excuses, such as the possibility that Paul might be an anti-Semite and therefore unworthy of calling, for the world to preach the Gospel to the Jews is nothing but nonsense. Another piece of drivel is the position that Jewish people do not need to hear about Jesus, because the original covenant was sufficient for their salvation. The time is now for Jewish evangelism, and the words and urgency found in 1 Thess 2:13–16 and Rom 9:1–5 are proof of this reality. So now that you have read these words, and perhaps even been reminded of other Pauline words such as "to the Jew first" (Rom 1:16), what are you going to do about them? Shalom!

---

3. Klassen, "Anti-Judaism in Early Christianity," 8; see also, Jocz, *Jesus Christ After Auschwitz*, 52–62, 152–67; and Jocz, *Church and Synagogue*, 314–22.

Bibliography

Aagaard, Johannes. "The Church and the Jews in Eschatology." *Lutheran World* 11, no. 3 (July 1964): 270-78.
Aageson, J. W. "Typology, Correspondence, and the Application of Scripture in Romans 9-11." *Journal for the Study of the New Testament* 31 (October 1987): 51-72.
Abasciano, Brian J. "Corporate Election in Romans 9: A Reply to Thomas Schreiner." *Journal of the Evangelical Theological Society* 49, no. 2 (June 2006): 351-71.
Aberbach, M. "The Conflicting Accounts of Josephus and Tacitus Concerning Cumanus' and Felix' Terms of Office." *Jewish Quarterly Review* 40, no. 1 (July 1949): 1-14.
Aland, Kurt, and Barbara Aland. *The Text of the New Testament: An Introduction to the Critical Editions and to the Theory and Practice of Modern Textual Criticism*. 2nd ed. Translated by Erroll F. Rhodes. Grand Rapids: Eerdmans, 1989.
Alston, Jr., Wallace M. "The Root that Supports Us." In *Removing Anti-Judaism from the Pulpit*, ed. Howard Clark Kee and Irvin J. Borowsky, 101-8. Philadelphia: American Interfaith Institute, 1996.
Anderson, Robert. "Re-Reading Paul: A Fresh Look at His Attitude to Torah and to Judaism." *Jewish Christian Relations* (May 1999) [position paper on-line]. Accessed September 15, 2006; available from www.jcrelations.net/en/index.php?id=789& format=print; Internet.
Aphrahat. "On the Peoples Which are in the Place of the People." In *Disputation and Dialogue: Readings in the Jewish-Christian Encounter*, ed. Frank Ephraim Talmage, 20-27. New York: KTAV Publishing House, 1975.
Augustine. "Reply to Faustus, the Manichean." In *Disputation and Dialogue: Readings in the Jewish-Christian Encounter*, ed. Frank Ephraim Talmage, 28-32. New York: KTAV Publishing House, 1975.
Aust, H., and D. Müller. "Curse, Insult, Fool (ajnavqema)." In *New International Dictionary of New Testament Theology*. Vol. 1. Edited by Colin Brown, 413-15. Grand Rapids: Zondervan Publishing House, 1976.
Baarda, Tjitze. "The Shechem Episode in the Testament of Levi: A Comparison of Other Traditions." In *Sacred History and Sacred Texts in Early Judaism: A Symposium in Honour of A. S. van der Woude*, ed. J. N. Bremmer and F. García Martínez, 11-73. Kampen: Kok Pharos, 1992.
Balz, H. "εὔχομαι." In *Exegetical Dictionary of the New Testament*, vol. 2, ed. Horst Balz and Gerhard Schneider, 88-89. Grand Rapids: Eerdmans, 1991.
———. "συμφορτίζω." In *Exegetical Dictionary of the New Testament*, vol. 3, ed. Horst Balz and Gerhard Schneider, 290. Grand Rapids: Eerdmans, 1991.
———. "λατρεία." In *Exegetical Dictionary of the New Testament*, vol. 2, ed. Horst Balz and Gerhard Schneider, 344-45. Grand Rapids: Eerdmans, 1991.

Barnhouse, Donald Grey. *God's Covenants: Exposition of Bible Doctrines, Taking the Epistles to the Romans as a Point of Departure*. Vol. 8. Grand Rapids: Eerdmans, 1963.

Barth, Karl. *The Epistle to the Romans*. 6th ed. Translated by Edwyn C. Hoskins. London: Oxford University Press, 1933.

Batheja, Aman. "Counterprotests Drown out Westboro Baptist Members at 2 Arlington Churches" [on-line]. Accessed 12 July 2010; available from http://www.star-telegram.com/2010/07/11/v-print/2327719/counterprotests-drown-out-westboro.html; Internet.

Bauer, Walter. *A Greek-English Lexicon of the New Testament and Other Early Christian Literature*. Edited and translated by William F. Arndt and Wilbur Gingrich. Chicago: University of Chicago Press, 1957.

Baum, Gregory. "Rethinking the Church's Mission after Auschwitz." In *Auschwitz: Beginning of a New Era? Reflections on the Holocaust*, ed. Eva Fleischner, 113–28. New York: KTAV Publishing House, 1977.

Baur, Ferdinand Christian. *Paul: The Apostle of Jesus, His Life and Work, His Epistles and His Doctrine, A Contribution to the Critical History of Primitive Christianity*. Vol. 2. Edited by Eduard Zeller and translated by A. Menzies. London: Williams & Norgate, 1875.

Beker, J. Christiaan. *Suffering and Hope: The Biblical Vision and the Human Predicament*. Grand Rapids: Eerdmans, 1994.

———. *The Triumph of God: The Essence of Paul's Thought*. Translated by Loren T. Struckenbruck. Minneapolis: Fortress, 1990.

———. "Romans 9–11 in the Context of the Early Church." *Princeton Seminary Bulletin*, Supplementary Issue No. 1 (1990): 40–55.

———. "The Faithfulness of God and the Priority of Israel in Paul's Letter to the Romans." *Harvard Theological Review* 79, nos. 1–3 (1986): 10–16.

Bell, Richard H. *Provoked to Jealousy: The Origin and Purpose of the Jealousy Motif in Romans 9–11*. Wissenschaftliche Untersuchungen zum Neuen Testament. Edited by Joachim Jeremias, et al. Tübingen: J. C. B. Mohr [Paul Siebeck], 1994.

Best, Ernest. *The First and Second Epistles to the Thessalonians*. Harper's New Testament Commentaries. Edited by Henry Chadwick. London: A. F. & C. Black, 1986. Reprint, Peabody, MA: Hendrickson Publishers, 1988.

Black, David Allen. *Learn to Read New Testament Greek: Expanded Edition*. Nashville: Broadman & Holman, 1994.

Blaising, Craig A. "The Future of Israel as a Theological Question." *Journal of the Evangelical Theological Society* 44, no. 3 (September 2001): 435–50.

Bloesch, Donald G. "'All Israel Will Be Saved': Supersessionism and the Biblical Witness." *Interpretation* 43, no. 2 (April 1989): 130–42.

Bockmuehl, Markus. "1 Thessalonians 2:14–16 and the Church in Jerusalem." *Tyndale Bulletin* 52, no. 1 (2001): 1–31.

Boers, Hendrikus. "The Form Critical Study of Paul's Letters: 1 Thessalonians as a Case Study." *New Testament Studies* 22 (1976): 140–58.

Brändle, Rudolf, and Ekkehard W. Stegemann. "The Formation of the First 'Christian Congregations' in Rome in the Context of the Jewish Congregations." In *Judaism and Christianity in First-Century Rome*, ed. Karl P. Donfried and Peter Richardson, 117–27. Grand Rapids: Eerdmans, 1998.

Bray, Gerald, ed. *Romans*. Ancient Christian Commentary on Scripture. Vol. 6. Downers Grove, IL: InterVarsity Press, 1998.

Bibliography

Breidenthal, Thomas. "Neighbor-Christology: Reconstructing Christianity Before Supersessionism." *Cross Currents* 49, no. 3 (Fall 1999): 319-48.
Brisco, Thomas V. *Holman Bible Atlas: A Complete Guide to the Expansive Geography of Biblical History.* Nashville: Holman Reference, 1998.
Brown, C. "Prayer (proseuvcomai)." In *The New International Dictionary of New Testament Theology*, vol. 2, gen. ed. Colin Brown, 861-67. Grand Rapids: Zondervan Publishing House, 1976.
Brown, Raymond E. *Jesus: God and Man: Modern Biblical Reflections.* Milwaukee: Bruce Publishing Co., 1967.
Bruce, F. F. *The Letter of Paul to the Romans: An Introduction and Commentary.* Tyndale New Testament Commentaries. Edited by Leon Morris. Grand Rapids: Eerdmans, 1987.
———. *1 & 2 Thessalonians.* Word Biblical Commentary. Vol. 45, New Testament. Edited by Ralph P. Martin. Waco, TX: Word Books, 1982.
———. "The Romans Debate—Continued." *Bulletin of the John Rylands University Library of Manchester* 64, no. 2 (Spring 1982): 334-59.
Burghardt, Walter. "Response to Rosemary Ruether." In *Auschwitz: Beginning of a New Era? Reflections on the Holocaust*, ed. Eva Fleischner, 93-95. New York: KTAV Publishing House, 1977.
Byrne, Brendan. *Romans.* Sacra Pagina Series. Vol. 6. Edited by Daniel J. Harrington. Collegeville, MN: Liturgical Press, 1996.
Calvin, John. *Commentaries on the Epistle of Paul the Apostle to the Romans.* Translated and edited by John Owen. Grand Rapids: Eerdmans, 1955.
Campbell, Roderick. *Israel and the New Covenant.* Phillipsburg, NJ: Presbyterian and Reformed Publishing, 1954.
Campbell, W. S. "Israel." In *Dictionary of Paul and His Letters*, ed. Gerald F. Hawthorne and Ralph P. Martin, 441-46. Downers Grove, IL: InterVarsity Press, 1993.
Cargas, Harry James. "Christian Preaching after the Holocaust." In *Removing Anti-Judaism from the Pulpit*, ed. Howard Clark Kee and Irvin J. Borowsky, 43-49. Philadelphia: American Interfaith Institute, 1996.
Carmichael, Joel. *The Satanizing of the Jews: Origin and Development of Mystical Anti-Semitism.* New York: Fromm Publishing, 1992.
Cary, M., and H. H. Scullard. *A History of Rome: Down to the Reign of Constantine.* 3rd ed. New York: St. Martin's Press, 1985.
Chae, Daniel Jong-Sang. *Paul as Apostle to the Gentiles: His Apostolic Self-Awareness and its Influence on the Soteriological Argument in Romans.* Paternoster Biblical and Theological Monographs. Carlisle, UK: Paternoster Press, 1997.
Cohn-Sherbok, Dan. *The Crucified Jew: Twenty Centuries of Christian Anti-Semitism.* Grand Rapids: Eerdmans; Philadelphia: American Interfaith Institute and the World Alliance of Interfaith Organizations, 1997.
Cook, James I. "The Christian Witness to the Jews: A Biblical Perspective for the Church Today." *Scottish Journal of Theology* 36, no. 2 (1983): 145-61.
Corley, Bruce. "The Significance of Romans 9-11: A Study in Pauline Theology." Ph.D. diss., Southwestern Baptist Theological Seminary, 1975.
Cranfield, C. E. B. *A Critical and Exegetical Commentary on the Epistle to the Romans.* International Critical Commentary. Vol. 2. Edited by J. A. Emerton, C. E. B. Cranfield, and G. N. Stanton. London: T. & T. Clark, 1979.

Bibliography

Cranford, Michael. "Election and Ethnicity: Paul's View of Israel in Romans 9.1–13." *Journal for the Study of the New Testament* 50 (June 1993): 27–41.

Das, A. Andrew. *Paul and the Jews.* Peabody, MA: Hendrickson Publishers, 2003.

Davidson, Robert. "Covenant Ideology in Ancient Israel." In *The World of Ancient Israel: Sociological, Anthropological and Political Perspectives,* ed. R. E. Clements, 323–47. Cambridge: Cambridge University Press, 1989.

Denney, James. *St. Paul's Epistle to the Romans.* Expositor's Greek Testament. Vol. 2. Edited by W. Robertson Nicoll. New York: George H. Doran, n.d.

Diprose, Ronald E. *Israel and the Church: The Origins and Effects of Replacement Theology.* Waynesboro, GA: Authentic Media, 2004.

Dodd, Brian J. *The Problem with Paul.* Downers Grove, IL: InterVarsity Press, 1996.

Donfried, Karl Paul. *Paul, Thessalonica, and Early Christianity.* Grand Rapids: Eerdmans, 2002.

———. "The Cults of Thessalonica and the Thessalonians Correspondence." *New Testament Studies* 31 (1985): 336–56.

———. "Paul and Judaism: 1 Thessalonians 2:13–16 as a Test Case." *Interpretation* 3 (July 1984): 242–53.

Downey, Amy. "An Apologetic Response on How to Share the Gospel of Messiah Jesus in Light of the Holocaust." Academic paper presented at the International Society of Christian Apologetics (ISCA), Fort Worth, Texas, 24 April 2010 [on-line]. Available from http://www.isca-apologetics.org/node/226; Internet.

Dunn, James D. G. "Judaism and Christianity: One Covenant or Two?: Chaplaincy Lecture." In *Covenant Theology: Contemporary Approaches,* ed. Mark J. Cartledge and David Mills, 33–55. Carlisle, UK: Paternoster Press, 2001.

———. "Romans, Letter to the." In *Dictionary of Paul and His Letters,* ed. Gerald F. Hawthorne *et al.,* 838–50. Downers Grove, IL: InterVarsity Press, 1993.

———. *Romans 9–16.* Word Biblical Commentary. Vol. 38a. New Testament. Edited by Ralph P. Martin. Dallas: Word Books, 1988.

Eichrodt, Walther. *Theology of the Old Testament.* Vol. 1. Translated by J. A. Baker. Philadelphia: Westminster, 1961.

Ellis, E. Earle. *Pauline Theology: Ministry and Society.* Grand Rapids: Eerdmans, 1989.

———. *Paul's Use of the Old Testament.* Grand Rapids: Baker, 1981. Reprint, Eugene, OR: Wipf and Stock Publishers, 1981.

Epp, Eldon Jay. "Jewish-Gentile Continuity in Paul: Torah and/or Faith? (Romans 9:1–5)." *Harvard Theological Review* 79, nos. 1–3 (1986): 80–90.

Ericksen, Robert P. *Theologians Under Hitler.* New Haven, CT: Yale University Press, 1985.

"Extremism in America—Westboro Baptist Church: About WBC" [on-line]. Accessed 10 June 2010; available from http://www.adl.org/learn/ext_us/WBC/default.asp?LEARN_Cat=Extremism&LEARN_SubCat=Extremism_in_America&xpicked=3&item=WBC; Internet.

Fasching, Darrell J. *Narrative Theology After Auschwitz: From Alienation to Ethics.* Minneapolis: Fortress, 1992.

Fee, Gordon D. *New Testament Exegesis: A Handbook for Students and Pastors.* 3rd ed. Louisville: Westminster/John Knox Press, 2002.

Ferguson, John. *The Religions of the Roman Empire.* Aspects of Greek and Roman Life. Edited by H. H. Scullard. Ithaca, NY: Cornell University Press, 1970.

Bibliography

Fisher, Eugene J. *Faith Without Prejudice: Rebuilding Christian Attitudes Toward Judaism.* Shared Ground Among Jews and Christians. Vol. 4. Rev. and exp. ed. New York: Crossroad Publishing, 1977.

Fitzmyer, Joseph A. *Romans: A New Translation with Introduction and Commentary.* Anchor Bible. Edited by William Albright and David Freedman. New York: Doubleday, 1993.

Forestell, J. Terence. *The Letters to the Thessalonians (1 Thess).* Jerome Biblical Commentary. Vol. 2. Edited by Raymond E. Brown, Joseph A. Fitzmyer, and Roland E. Murphy. Englewood Cliffs, NJ: Prentice-Hall, 1968.

Fraikin, Daniel. "The Rhetorical Function of the Jews in Romans." In *Anti-Judaism in Early Christianity.* Vol. 1. Paul and the Gospels: Studies in Christianity and Judaism, ed. Peter Richardson, 91–106. Canada: Wilfrid Laurier University Press, 1986.

Frame, James Everett. *A Critical and Exegetical Commentary on the Epistles of St. Paul to the Thessalonians.* International Critical Commentary. Edited by S. R. Driver, Alfred Plummer, and Charles A. Briggs. Edinburgh: T. & T. Clark, 1912.

Freudmann, Lillian C. *Antisemitism in the New Testament.* Lanham, MD: University Press of America, 1994.

Gaebelein, Frank E. *Romans—Galatians.* Expositor's Bible Commentary with the New International Version of the Holy Bible. Vol. 10. Grand Rapids: Zondervan Publishing House, 1976.

Gager, John G. *Reinventing Paul.* New York: Oxford University Press, 2000.

———. *The Origins of Anti-Semitism: Attitudes Toward Judaism in Pagan and Christian Antiquity.* New York: Oxford University Press, 1985.

Garrett, James Leo. *Systematic Theology.* Vol. 2. Grand Rapids: Eerdmans, 1995.

Gaston, Lloyd. "Israel's Missteps in the Eyes of Paul." In *The Romans Debate: Revised and Expanded Edition*, ed. Karl P. Donfried, 309–326. Peabody, MA: Hendrickson, 1977.

Gerdmar, Anders. *Roots of Theological Anti-Semitism: German Biblical Interpretation and the Jews, from Herder and Semler to Kittel and Bultman.* Studies in Jewish History and Culture, vol. 20. Leiden, The Netherlands: Koninklijke Brill NV, 2009.

Gilliard, Frank D. "Paul and the Killing of the Prophets in 1 Thess. 2:15." *Novum Testamentum* 36, no. 3 (1994): 259–70.

———. "The Problem of the Antisemitic Comma Between 1 Thessalonians 2.14 and 15." *New Testament Studies* 35 (1989): 481–502.

Grant, Michael. *History of Rome.* New York: Charles Scribner's Sons, 1978.

———. *The World of Rome.* Cleveland: World Publishing Co., 1960.

Greek New Testament (UBS). 4th ed. Stuttgart: Deutsche Bibelgesellschaft, 1993.

Green, Gene L. *The Letters to the Thessalonians.* Pillar New Testament Commentary. Edited by D. A. Carson. Grand Rapids: Eerdmans, 2002.

Gruen, Erich S. *Diaspora: Jews Amidst Greeks and Romans.* Cambridge, MA: Harvard University Press, 2002.

Guerra, Anthony J. "Romans: Paul's Purpose and Audience with Special Attention to Romans 9–11." *Revue Biblique* 97, no. 2 (1990): 219–37.

Haenchen, Ernst. *The Acts of the Apostles: A Commentary.* Translated by Bernard Noble and Gerald Shinn. Philadelphia: Westminster Press, 1971.

Hagee, John. *Jerusalem Countdown: A Warning to the World.* Lake Mary, FL: FrontLine, 2006.

Bibliography

Hagner, Donald A. "Paul's Quarrel with Judaism." In *Anti-Semitism and Early Christianity: Issues of Polemic and Faith*, ed. Craig A. Evans and Donald A. Hagner, 128–50. Minneapolis: Fortress, 1993.

Hall, III, Sidney G. *Christian Anti-Semitism and Paul's Theology*. Minneapolis: Fortress, 1993.

Hann, Robert R. "Supersessionism, Engraftment, and Jewish-Christian Dialogue: Reflections on the Presbyterian Statement on Jewish-Christian Relations." *Journal of Ecumenical Studies* 27, no. 2 (Spring 1990): 327–42.

Harrison, J. R. "Paul and the Imperial Gospel at Thessaloniki." *Journal for the Study of the New Testament* 25, no. 1 (2002): 71–96.

Hendriksen, William. *New Testament Commentary: Exposition of Paul's Epistle to the Romans*. Vol. 2. Grand Rapids: Baker Book House, 1981.

Hess, K. "latreiva." In *New International Dictionary of New Testament Theology*, vol. 3, ed. Colin Brown, 549–51. Grand Rapids: Zondervan Publishing House, 1978.

Hicks, John, et al. *The Federal Union: A History of the United States to 1877*. 5th ed. Boston: Houghton Mifflin Co., 1970.

Hiebert, D. Edmond. *The Thessalonian Epistles: A Call to Readiness*. Chicago: Moody Press, 1971.

Hillers, Delbert R. *Covenant: The History of a Biblical Idea*. Baltimore: Johns Hopkins Press, 1969.

Hodge, Charles. *Commentary on the Epistle to the Romans*. Grand Rapids: Eerdmans, 1955.

Holmes, Michael W. *1 and 2 Thessalonians*. NIV Application Commentary Series. Edited by Terry Muck. Grand Rapids: Zondervan Publishing House, 1998.

Holmstrand, Jonas. *Markers and Meaning in Paul: An Analysis of 1 Thessalonians, Philippians and Galatians*. Coniectanea Biblica New Testament Series 28. Stockholm: Almqvist & Wiksell International, 1997.

Holwerda, David E. *Jesus and Israel: One Covenant or Two?*. Grand Rapids: Eerdmans, 1995.

Horner, Barry E. *Future Israel: Why Christian Anti-Judaism Must Be Challenged*. NAC Studies in Bible & Theology. Edited by E. Ray Clendenen. Nashville: B & H Academic, 2007.

Huidekoper, Frederic. *Judaism at Rome: B. C. 76 to A. D. 140*. New York: James Miller, 1876.

Hurd, John C. "Paul Ahead of His Time: 1 Thess. 2:13-16." In *Anti-Judaism in Early Christianity*. Vol. 1. Paul and the Gospels: Studies in Christianity and Judaism, ed. Peter Richardson, 21–36. Canada: Wilfrid Laurier University Press, 1986.

"Interpolate" [on-line]. Accessed 11 July 2010; available from http://www.merriam-webster.com/dictionary/interpolate; Internet.

Jewett, Robert. "The Law and the Coexistence of Jews and Gentiles in Romans." *Interpretation* 39, no. 4 (October 1985): 342–56.

Jocz, Jacob. *The Jewish People and Jesus Christ After Auschwitz*. Grand Rapids: Baker Books, 1981.

———. *The Jewish People and Jesus Christ: A Study in the Controversy Between Church and Synagogue*. London: SPCK, 1954.

Johnson, E. Elizabeth. "Romans 9-11: The Faithfulness and Impartiality of God." In *Pauline Theology: Romans*, vol. 3, ed. David M. Hay and E. Elizabeth Johnson, 211–40. Minneapolis: Fortress, 1995.

Johnson, John J. "A New Testament Understanding of the Jewish Rejection of Jesus: Four Theologians on the Salvation of Israel." *Journal of the Evangelical Theological Society* 43, no. 2 (June 2000): 229–46.

Johnson, Luke Timothy. *Reading Romans: A Literary and Theological Commentary*. Macon, GA: Smyth & Helwys, 2001.

Johnson, Sherman E. "Jews and Christians in Rome." *Lexington Theology Quarterly* 17, no. 4 (October 1982): 51–58.

Jones, David W., and John K. Tarwater. "Are Biblical Covenants Dissoluble?" *Southwestern Journal of Theology* 47, no. 1 (Fall 2004): 1–11.

Jowett, Benjamin. *The Epistles of St. Paul to the Thessalonians, Galatians, Romans: With Critical Notes and Dissertations*. 2nd ed. Vol. 2. London: John Murray, 1859.

Judge, E. A. "The Decrees of Caesar at Thessalonica." *Reformed Theological Review* 30, no. 1 (January-April 1971): 1–7.

Kaylor, R. David. *Paul's Covenant Community: Jew and Gentile in Romans*. Atlanta: John Knox Press, 1988.

Kim, Johann D. *God, Israel, and the Gentiles: Rhetoric and Situation in Romans 9–11*. No. 176. Society of Biblical Literature Dissertation Series. Edited by Mark Allan Powell. Atlanta: Society of Biblical Literature, 2000.

Kinzer, Mark S. *Postmissionary Messianic Judaism: Redefining Christian Engagement with the Jewish People*. Grand Rapids: Brazos Press, 2005.

Kittel, Gerhard, ed. *Theological Dictionary of the New Testament*. Vol. 3. Translated by Geoffrey W. Bromiley. Grand Rapids: Eerdmans, 1965.

Klassen, William. "Anti-Judaism in Early Christianity: The State of the Question." In *Anti-Judaism in Early Christianity*. Paul and the Gospels: Studies in Christianity and Judaism, vol. 1, ed. Peter Richardson, 1–19. Waterloo, Ontario, Canada: Wilfrid Laurier University Press, 1986.

Klein, William W. *The New Chosen People: A Corporate View of Election*. Grand Rapids: Academie Books/Zondervan, 1990.

Kreloff, Steven A. *God's Plan for Israel: A Study of Romans 9–11*. Neptune, NJ: Loizeaux, 1995.

Kuhli, H. "Ἰουδαῖος." In *Exegetical Dictionary of the New Testament*, vol. 2, ed. Horst Balz and Gerhard Schneider, 193–97. Grand Rapids: Eerdmans, 1991.

Lamp, Jeffrey S. "Is Paul Anti-Jewish?: *Testament of Levi* 6 in the Interpretation of 1 Thessalonians 2:13–16." *Catholic Biblical Quarterly* 65 (2003): 408–27.

Lampe, Peter. *From Paul to Valentinus: Christians at Rome in the First Two Centuries*. Translated by Michael Steinhauser and edited Marshall D. Johnson. Minneapolis: Fortress, 2003.

Lattey, Cuthbert. "The Codex Ephraemi Rescriptus on Romans ix.5." *Expository Times* 35, no. 1 (October 1923): 42–43.

Lenski, R. C. H. *The Interpretation of St. Paul's Epistle to the Romans*. Columbus, OH: Wartburg Press, 1945.

Leon, Harry J. *The Jews of Ancient Rome*. Morris Loeb Series. No. 5. Philadelphia: Jewish Publication Society of America, 1960.

Levine, Amy-Jill. *The Misunderstood Jew: The Church and the Scandal of the Jewish Jesus*. New York: HarperOne, 2006.

Liddon, H. P. *Explanatory Analysis of St. Paul's Epistle to the Romans*. Grand Rapids: Zondervan Publishing House, 1961.

Littell, Franklin H. *The Crucifixion of the Jews*. Macon, GA: Mercer University Press, 1986; reprint from 1975 edition.

Lohfink, Norbert. *The Covenant Never Revoked: Biblical Reflections on Christian-Jewish Dialogue*. Translated by John J. Scullion. New York: Paulist Press, 1991.

Longenecker, Bruce W. "Different Answers to Different Issues: Israel, the Gentiles and Salvation History in Romans 9–11." *Journal for the Study of the New Testament* 36 (June 1989): 95–123.

MacArthur, John, Jr. *Romans 9–16*. MacArthur New Testament Commentary. Chicago: Moody Press, 1994.

Malherbe, Abraham J. *The Letter to the Thessalonians: A New Translation with Introduction and Commentary*. Anchor Bible. Vol. 32b. Edited by William Foxwell Albright and David Noel Freedman. New York: Doubleday, 2000.

———. *Paul and the Thessalonians: The Philosophic Tradition of Pastoral Care*. Philadelphia: Fortress, 1987.

Manus, Chris Ukachukwu. "Luke's Account of Paul in Thessalonica (Acts 17, 1–9)." In *Thessalonian Correspondence*. Bibliotheca Ephemeridum Theologicarum Lovaniensium, vol. 87, ed. Raymond F. Collins, 27–38. Leuven: University Press, 1990.

Marshall, I. Howard. *1 and 2 Thessalonians: Based on the Revised Standard Version*. New Century Bible Commentary. Edited by Matthew Black. Grand Rapids: Eerdmans, 1983.

Martin, D. Michael. *1, 2 Thessalonians*. New American Commentary. Vol. 33. Edited by E. Ray Clendenen. Nashville: Broadman and Holman, 1995.

Martyr, Justin. "Dialogue with Trypho." In *Disputation and Dialogue: Readings in the Jewish-Christian Encounter*, ed. Frank Ephraim Talmage, 92–99. New York: KTAV Publishing House, 1975.

Mayer, R. "Israel, Jew, Hebrew, Jacob, Judah." In *New International Dictionary of New Testament Theology*, vol. 2, ed. Colin Brown, 304–16. Grand Rapids: Zondervan Publishing House, 1976.

McCarthy, Dennis J. *Old Testament Covenant: A Survey of Current Opinions*. Richmond, VA: John Knox, 1972.

Meeks, Wayne A. *The First Urban Christians: The Social World of the Apostle Paul*. New Haven, CT: Yale University Press, 1983.

———. *The Writings of St. Paul: A Norton Critical Edition: Annotated Text Criticism*. New York: W. W. Norton & Co., 1972.

Meeks, Wayne A., and Robert L. Wilken. *Jews and Christians in Antioch in the First Four Centuries of the Common Era*. No. 13. Society of Biblical Literature Sources for Bible Study. Edited by Wayne A. Meeks. Missoula, MT: Scholars Press, 1978.

Metzger, Bruce M. *The Text of the New Testament: Its Transmission, Corruption, and Restoration*. 3rd ed. New York: Oxford University Press, 1992.

———. *A Textual Commentary on the Greek New Testament: A Companion Volume to the United Bible Societies' Greek New Testament*. 3rd ed. London: United Bible Societies, 1975.

———. "The Punctuation of Rom. 9:5." In *Christ and the Spirit in the New Testament*. Edited by Barnabas Lindars and Stephen S. Smalley, 95–112. Cambridge: University Press, 1973.

Milligan, George. *St. Paul's Epistles to the Thessalonians: The Greek Text with Introduction and Notes*. Grand Rapids: Eerdmans, 1953.

Moffatt, James. *The First and Second Epistles to the Thessalonians*. Expositor's Greek Testament. Vol. 4. Edited by W. Robertson Nicoll. Reprint ed. Grand Rapids: Eerdmans, 1980.

Moo, Douglas J. *The Epistle to the Romans*. Grand Rapids: Eerdmans, 1996.

Morris, Leon. *The Epistle to the Romans*. Grand Rapids: Eerdmans, 1988.

Moule, C. F. D. *The Birth of the New Testament*. 2nd ed. London: Adam and Charles Black, 1966.

Munck, Johannes. *Christ and Israel: An Interpretation of Romans 9–11*. Philadelphia: Fortress, 1967.

Murrell, N. Samuel, "The Human Paul of the New Testament: Anti-Judaism in 1 Thess 2:14–16." *Proceedings* 14 (1994): 169–87.

Nash, Henry S. "Interpolations in the New Testament" [on-line]. Accessed 11 July 2010; available from http://www.ccel.org/s/schaff/encyc06/htm/iii.xi.htm; Internet.

Nicholson, Ernest W. *God and His People: Covenant and Theology in the Old Testament*. Oxford: Clarendon Press, 1986.

Okeke, G. E. "I Thessalonians 2.13–16: The Fate of the Unbelieving Jews." *New Testament Studies* 27 (1981): 127–36.

Osborne, Grant R. *Romans*. IVP New Testament Commentary Series. Edited by Grant R. Osborne. Downers Grove, IL: InterVarsity Press, 2004.

Papachristou, Henry, and Kyriakidou, Dina. "Vandals Desecrate Jewish Cemetery in Greece" [on-line]. Accessed May 14, 2010; available from http://www.reuters.com/assets/print? aid=USTRE64D4ZB20100514; Internet.

Patte, Daniel. "Anti-Semitism in the New Testament: Confronting the Dark Side of Paul's and Matthew's Teaching." *Chicago Theological Seminary Register* 77, no. 1 (Winter 1988): 31–52.

Pauck, Wilhelm, trans. and ed. *Luther: Lectures on Romans*. In Library of Christian Classics. Vol. 15. Edited by John Baillie. Philadelphia: Westminster Press, 1961.

Pearson, Birger A. "1 Thessalonians 2:13–16: A Deutero-Pauline Interpolation." *Harvard Theological Review* 64 (1971): 79–94.

Piper, John. *The Justification of God: An Exegetical and Theological Study of Romans 9:1–23*. Grand Rapids: Baker, 1993.

Plumer, William S. *Commentary on Romans*. Grand Rapids: Kregel Publications, 1971.

Riesner, Rainer. *Paul's Early Period: Chronology, Mission Strategy, Theology*. Translated by Doug Stott. Grand Rapids: Eerdmans, 1998.

Robertson, Archibald Thomas. *Word Pictures in the New Testament*. Vol. 4. Epistles of Paul. Nashville: Broadman, 1931.

Robinson, D. W. B. "The Salvation of Israel in Romans 9–11." *Reformed Theological Review* 26, no. 3 (September/December 1967): 81–96.

Roetzel, Calvin. "Diaqh`kai in Romans 9, 4." *Biblica: Commentarii Periodici Pontificii Instituti Biblici* 51, fasc. 3 (1970): 377–90.

Rowley, H. H. *The Biblical Doctrine of Election*. London: Lutterworth Press, 1950.

Ruether, Rosemary Radford. *Faith and Fratricide: The Theological Roots of Anti-Semitism*. New York: Seabury Press, 1974.

Rutgers, Leonard Victor. "Roman Policy Toward the Jews: Expulsions from the City of Rome During the First Century C.E." In *Judaism and Christianity in First Century Rome*, ed. Karl P. Donfried and Peter Richardson, 93–116. Grand Rapids: Eerdmans, 1998.

Rydelnik, Michael. "Was Paul Anti-Semitic?: Revisiting 1 Thessalonians 2:14–16." *Bibliotheca Sacra* 185 (January-March 2008): 58–67.

Sanday, William, and Arthur C. Headlam. *A Critical and Exegetical Commentary on the Epistle to the Romans*. International Critical Commentary. 5th ed. Edinburgh: T. & T. Clark, 1980.

Sanders, E. P. *Paul, the Law, and the Jewish People*. Philadelphia: Fortress, 1983.

Sandmel, Samuel. *Anti-Semitism in the New Testament?*. Philadelphia: Fortress, 1978.

Saperstein, Marc. *Moments in Crisis in Jewish-Christian Relations*. London: SCM Press; Philadelphia: Trinity Press International, 1989.

Schippers, R. "The Pre-Synoptic Tradition in 1 Thessalonians II 13–16." *Novum Testamentum*, 8, fasc. 2–4 (April-October 1966): 223–34.

Schlatter, Adolf. *Romans: The Righteousness of God*. Translated by Siegfried S. Schatzmann. Peabody, MA: Hendrickson Publishers, 1995.

Schmidt, Daryl. "1 Thess. 2:13–16: Linguistic Evidence for an Interpolation." *Journal of Biblical Literature* 102, no. 2 (June 1983): 269–79.

Schreiner, Thomas. "Corporate and Individual Election in Romans 9: A Response to Brian Abasciano." *Journal of the Evangelical Theological Society* 49, no. 2 (June 2006): 373–86.

―――. *Paul: Apostle of God's Glory in Christ: A Pauline Theology*. Downers Grove, IL: InterVarsity Press, 2001.

―――. *Romans*. Baker Exegetical Commentary on the New Testament. Grand Rapids: Baker, 1998.

―――. "Does Romans 9 Teach Individual Election Unto Salvation? Some Exegetical and Theological Reflections." *Journal of the Evangelical Theology Society* 36, no. 1 (March 1993): 25–40.

Schwier, Helmut, ed. "Church and Israel: A Contribution from the Reformation Churches in Europe to the Relationship Between Christians and Jews." *Jewish-Christian Relations* 1009 (July 2001) [position paper on-line]. Accessed September 15, 2006; available from http:// www.jcrelations.net/en/index.php?id=1009&format=print; Internet.

Scott, J. M. "Restoration of Israel." In *Dictionary of Paul and His Letters*, ed. Gerald F. Hawthorne, et al., 797–805. Downers Grove, IL: InterVarsity Press, 1993.

Shedd, William G. T. *Commentary on Romans*. Grand Rapids: Baker Book House, 1980; reprint from 1879 edition.

Shimkus, Craig Thomas. "*Adversus Ioudaeos*: The Development of a Polemic Against the Jews 100–400 C.E." MA.Th. thesis, Southwestern Baptist Theological Seminary, 2000.

Shulevitz, Judith. "Was Paul a Jew?: A New Generation of Scholars Argues that the Apostle Long Considered the Progenitor of Anti-Semitism Never Left His Religion" [on-line]. Accessed 10 July 2010; available from http://www.tabletmag.com/arts-and-culture/books/20214/who-was-paul/; Internet.

Siker, Jeffrey S. *Disinheriting the Jews: Abraham in Early Christian Controversy*. Louisville: Westminster/John Knox, 1991.

Simpson, John W., Jr. "The Problems Posed by 1 Thessalonians 2:15–16 and a Solution." *Horizons in Biblical Theology* 12, no. 1 (June 1990): 42–72.

Sneen, Donald. "The Root, the Remnant, and the Branches." *Word and World* 6, no. 4 (1986): 398–409.

Soulen, R. Kendall. *The God of Israel and Christian Theology*. Minneapolis: Fortress, 1996.

Bibliography

Steele, E. Springs. "Jewish Scriptures in 1 Thessalonians." *Biblical Theology Bulletin* 14, no. 1 (January 1984): 12–17.

Stendahl, Krister. *Final Account: Paul's Letter to the Romans*. Minneapolis: Fortress, 1995.

Still, Todd. *Conflict at Thessalonica: A Pauline Church and Its Neighbours*. Journal for the Study of the New Testament. Supplement Series 183. Edited by Stanley E. Porter. Sheffield: Sheffield Academic Press, 1999.

———. "Paul's Thessalonian Mission." *Southwestern Journal of Theology* 42, no. 1 (Fall 1999): 4–16.

———. *Paul Among Jews and Gentiles and Other Essays*. Philadelphia: Fortress, 1976.

Stowers, Stanley K. *A Rereading of Romans: Justice, Jews, and Gentiles*. New Haven, CT: Yale University Press, 1994.

Strathmann, "λατρεία." In *Theological Dictionary of the New Testament*, ed. Gerhard Kittel and trans. Geoffrey Bromiley, 58–65. Grand Rapids: Eerdmans, 1967.

Stuhlmacher, Peter. *Paul's Letter to the Romans: A Commentary*. Translated by Scott J. Hafemann. Louisville: Westminster/John Knox Press, 1994.

Taylor, Nicholas H. "Who Persecuted the Thessalonian Christians?" *Hervormde Teologiese Studies* 58, no. 2 (June 2002): 784–801.

Tellbe, Mikael. *Paul Between Synagogue and State: Christians, Jews, and Civic Authorities in 1 Thessalonians, Romans, and Philippians*. Coniectanea Biblica New Testament Series 34. Stockholm: Almqvist & Wiksell International, 2001.

Telushkin, Joseph. *Jewish Literacy: The Most Important Things to Know About the Jewish Religion, Its People, and Its History*. New York: William Morrow and Co., 1991.

Thielman, Frank. "Unexpected Mercy: Echoes of a Biblical Motif in Romans 9–11." *Scottish Journal of Theology* 47, no. 2 (1994): 169–81.

Tuckett, C. M. "Synoptic Tradition in 1 Thessalonians." In *Thessalonian Correspondence*. Bibliotheca Ephemeridum Theologicarum Lovaniensium, vol. 87, ed. Raymond F. Collins, 160–82. Leuven: University Press, 1990.

Van Buren, Paul M. "The Problem of a Christian Theology of the People Israel." *NICM Journal* 7 (Spring 1982): 47–64.

Wagner, J. Ross. *Heralds of the Good News: Isaiah and Paul "In Concert" in the Letter to the Romans*. Supplements to Novum Testamentum. Vol. CI. Edited by M. M. Mitchell and D. P. Moessner. Leiden: Brill, 2002.

Wakefield, Andrew. "Romans 9–11: The Sovereignty of God and the Status of Israel." *Review and Expositor* 100 (Winter 2003): 65–80.

Wallace, Daniel B. *Greek Grammar: Beyond the Basics: An Exegetical Syntax of the New Testament*. Grand Rapids: Zondervan, 1996.

Walters, James C. *Ethnic Issues in Paul's Letter to the Romans: Changing Self-Definitions in Earliest Roman Christianity*. Valley Forge, PA: Trinity Press International, 1993.

Wanamaker, Charles A. *The Epistles to the Thessalonians: A Commentary on the Greek Text*. New International Greek Testament Commentary. Edited by I. Howard Marshall and W. Ward Gasque. Grand Rapids: Eerdmans, 1990.

Wasserberg, Günter. "Romans 9–11 and Jewish-Christian Dialogue: Prospects and Provisos." In *Reading Israel in Romans: Legitimacy and Plausibility of Divergent Interpretations*. Edited by Cristina Grenholm and Daniel Patte, 174–86. Harrisburg, PA: Trinity Press International, 2000.

Weatherly, Jon A. "The Authenticity of 1 Thessalonians 2.13–16: Additional Evidence." *Journal for the Study of the New Testament* 42 (1991): 79–98.

Weinfeld. "*Berith.*" In *Theological Dictionary of the Old Testament*, vol. 2 ed. G. Johannes Botterweck and Helmer Ringgren and translated by John T. Willis, 253–79. Grand Rapids: Eerdmans, 1975.

"Westboro Baptist Church: About WBC." Anti-Defamation League [on-line]. Accessed July 12, 2010; available from http://www.adl.org/learn/ext_us/WBC/default.asp?LEARN_Cat=Extremism&LEARN_SubCat=Extremism_in_America&xpicked=3&item=WBC; Internet.

Westenholz, Joan Goodnick, ed. *The Jewish Presence in Ancient Rome*. Jerusalem: Bible Lands Museum, 1995.

Willert, Niels. "The Catalogues of Hardships in the Pauline Correspondence: Background and Function." In *The New Testament and Hellenistic Judaism*, ed. Peder Borgen and Søren Giverson, 217–43. Peabody, MA: Hendrickson Publishers, 1995.

Williams, David J. *1 and 2 Thessalonians*. New International Biblical Commentary. Peabody, MA: Hendrickson Publishers, 1992.

Williamson, Clark M. *A Guest in the House of Israel: Post-Holocaust Church Theology*. Louisville: Westminster/John Knox Press, 1993.

———. *Has God Rejected His People?: Anti-Judaism in the Christian Church*. Nashville: Abingdon, 1982.

Williamson, Clark M., and Ronald J. Allen. "Interpreting Difficult Texts." In *Removing Anti-Judaism from the Pulpit*, ed. Howard Clark Kee and Irvin J. Borowsky, 36–42. Philadelphia: American Interfaith Institute, 1996.

Willimon, William H. "Jews and Christians: All in the Family." In *Removing Anti-Judaism from the Pulpit*, ed. Howard Clark Kee and Irvin J. Borowsky, 121–26. Philadelphia: American Interfaith Institute, 1996.

Willis, Garry. *What Paul Meant*. New York: Viking Adult, 2006.

Wilson, Marvin R. *Our Father Abraham: Jewish Roots of the Christian Faith*. Dayton, OH: Center for Judaic-Christian Studies, 1989.

Wilson, Stephen C. *Related Strangers: Jews and Christians*. Minneapolis: Augsburg Fortress, 2004.

Witherington, Ben, III, and Darlene Hyatt. *Paul's Letter to the Romans: A Socio-Rhetorical Commentary*. Grand Rapids: Eerdmans, 2004.

Wortham, Robert A. "The Problem of Anti-Judaism in 1 Thess. 2:14–16 and Related Pauline Texts." *Biblical Theology Bulletin* 25, no. 1 (Spring 1995): 37–44.

Wright, N. T. *The Climax of the Covenant: Christ and the Law in Pauline Theology*. Minneapolis: Fortress, 1991.

Young, Brad H. *Paul the Jewish Theologian: A Pharisee Among Christians, Jews, and Gentiles*. Peabody, MA: Hendrickson Publishers, 1997.

Index

Acts 17, 8, 8n9, 9, 9n15, 10, 11
Anti-Semitism, 4, 4n14, 12, 28,
   29n34, 37n3, 61–68, 86n36, 88

Covenant, 29, 51–52, 51n92, 52n95

Decrees of Caesar, 8, 8n8
Dual Covenant (al) (alism), 4, 4n16,
   21, 38, 39n9, 43n41, 44, 69–78,
   79n1, 80, 83, 85n31

Holocaust (aka Shoah), 2, 37, 57,
   62, 65, 72, 72n10, 74n20, 77,
   77n32, 79n1, 80, 92

Jesus, Jesus the Messiah, Messiah
   Jesus, Jesus Christ, 1, 4n17, 6,
   10, 15, 26, 27, 29–34, 35n75,
   37n3, 39, 40, 42, 43, 44, 45,
   47n68, 49, 53–57, 59, 62–64,
   66, 66n28, 69, 71–73, 73n15,
   74, 74n20, 75, 75n21, 76–79,
   81, 83–93
Jewish Evangelism, 19, 33, 38, 59, 65,
   77, 77n32, 91–93, 92n2
Jewish Population in Thessalonica
   and/or Rome, 9, 10, 29

Moses, 40, 44, 52, 52n95, 56, 69, 71,
   76

Oath Formula/Statement, 39–40,
   40–44

Paul, Epistles (Letters) of, 1, 5, 7,
   11–12, 13, 18–20, 19n37, 23,
   35, 65
Paul, Evangelist (Missionary) to the
   Gentiles, 1, 10, 10n20, 11, 18,
   26, 30, 32, 44, 44n45, 66n29,
   70, 72–73, 75n22, 77, 83, 84,
   86, 86n39, 92
Paul, student of Gamaliel, 1, 25, 90

Replacement Theology (aka
   Supercessionism), 4, 4n17,
   21, 37–38, 37n3, 48, 54n114,
   70n1, 75n25, 76n27, 79–89,
   91, 92
Romans 1:16, 13, 19, 29, 93
Romans 9:1–5, 2, 3, 4, 16, 19n37,
   20, 21, 27, 33, 37–57, 69–78,
   79–89, 90, 92, 93
Romans 9–11, 2, 13, 19, 33, 36n76,
   37, 38, 65
Rome (an Church), 3, 5, 7, 13–17, 18,
   19, 90
Rome, Jewish Influence, 14–17

Self-Hating Jew (Paul's Relationship
   to the Jewish People?), 1, 2, 4,
   10n17, 29, 32, 37
Suffering (symbol of Christian
   faith), 9n15, 10, 26–27, 27–28,
   28n29, 43, 44, 63
Synagogue Worship, 9, 9n13, 10,
   10n20, 16n22, 17–18, 17n29,
   38, 61n2, 83n21

Thessalonica (ian Church), 3, 5, 7, 8, 9n13, 10–12, 13, 23–25, 27, 28, 28n29, 34, 66

Thessalonica, Jewish Influence, 9, 10

Thessalonians, First, 2:13–16, 2–4, 9, 21, 23–36, 61–68, 90, 91, 92

Thessalonians, First, 2:13–16, Interpolation, 21, 26, 27, 31, 32, 36n76, 61–68, 92

Wrath (of God), 32, 33, 34–36, 34n69, 36n78, 47, 63–66, 66n28, 91

www.ingramcontent.com/pod-product-compliance
Lightning Source LLC
Chambersburg PA
CBHW070928160426
43193CB00011B/1618